Praise for *I Came to Cast Fire*

"*I Came to Cast Fire* is a comprehensive yet short and accessible introduction to the world of René Girard, casting a new light on the wise sage whose recognition is growing with each year. Every page reflects not only Girard's genius, but also the learned, wise, and eloquent author behind the book, Fr. Elias Carr. Perhaps most importantly for reaching a general audience, *I Came to Cast Fire* is, above all, an enjoyable read."

—**Cynthia L. Haven**, National Endowment for the Humanities Public Scholar and author of *Evolution of Desire: A Life of René Girard*

"Fr. Elias Carr has produced an engaging introduction to the life and thought of René Girard. Through anecdotes and practical examples, he makes Girard's work accessible to newcomers and provides fresh insights for those already familiar with this towering intellect. As Fr. Elias reminds us, René Girard's work is a timely interpretive key to understanding human history, the challenges of today's culture, and our need for conversion to Christ."

—**Bishop Robert J. McClory**, Diocese of Gary

"With *I Came to Cast Fire*, Fr. Elias Carr announces himself as one of the premier communicators of René Girard's mimetic theory. Fr. Elias provides everything one looks for in an introduction: clarity, precision, brevity, breadth, and accuracy. He manages to guide the reader on a patient and succinct tour through Girard's thought and its relationship to the Gospel, one that never feels rushed or careless. Fr. Elias even provides personal anecdotes that show how mimetic theory has helped him make sense of his life and priestly vocation. I highly recommend this book for anyone eager to learn what René Girard's work has to do with their faith and their life."

—**Grant Kaplan**, Professor of Systematic and Historical Theology, Saint Louis University

"In the writings of René Girard, the French genius, we find a dithyrambic deluge of chthonic thought and ouranic ecstasy. In *I Came to Cast Fire*, Dom Elias Carr channels the torrent into a drink-size portion for twenty-first-century Anglophones. Well done, Father!"

—**Bishop Kurt Burnette**, Eparch of Passaic

"*I Came to Cast Fire* is much more than an introduction to René Girard's mimetic theory. It provides a personal, engaging, and insightful theological interpretation of mimetic desire and scapegoating, especially within modernity. Fr. Elias highlights, in an accessible and energetic manner, the relevance of Girard's insights for fundamental questions of human life and the proclamation of the Gospel. Rather than 'fade away,' as Fr. Elias suggests about himself after introducing Girard, I hope that this is only the beginning, and that we can look forward to further reflections on Christian humanism and the connections between the human sciences and Catholic theology."

—**Clemens Cavallin**, Professor of Christianity, Religion, Philosophies of Life, and Ethics, NLA University College (Bergen, Norway)

I CAME TO CAST FIRE

I CAME TO CAST FIRE

An Introduction to René Girard

Fr. Elias Carr

Foreword by Luke Burgis

Published by Word on Fire, Elk Grove Village, IL 60007
© 2024 by Fr. Elias Carr
Printed in the United States of America
All rights reserved

Cover design by Michael Stevens

Typesetting and interior art direction by
Katherine Spitler and Rozann Lee

Scripture excerpts are from the New Revised Standard Version Bible: Catholic Edition (copyright © 1989, 1993), used by permission of the National Council of the Churches of Christ in the United States of America. All rights reserved worldwide.

No part of this book may be used or reproduced in any manner whatsoever without written permission, except in the case of brief quotations in critical articles or reviews. For more information, contact Word on Fire Catholic Ministries, PO Box 97330, Washington, DC 20090-7330 or email contact@wordonfire.org.

ISBN: 978-1-68578-166-8

Library of Congress Control Number: 2024938882

Contents

Foreword by Luke Burgis ix

Introduction: The Day I Discovered Girard 1

1: Meet René Noël Théophile Girard 5

2: The Big Question 14

3: Mimetic Desire: That Which Is Truly Ours 18

4: The Romantic Lie: "I Am an Original" 31

5: The Right and Wrong Distance: External and
   Internal Mediation 34

6: Mimetic Rivalry: When Desire Goes Wrong 39

7: The Scapegoat 44

8: The Scapegoat Mechanism 48

9: The Founding Murder 52

10: The Foundations of Culture: Ritual Sacrifice, Myth,
    and Prohibition 56

11: The Old Testament on the Kingdom and the Temple 65

12: The Resurrection Reveals the Scapegoat Mechanism
    and the Innocence of the Victim 72

13: The Holy Spirit, the Paraclete 79

14: The Age of the Gentiles (Nations) 83

15: "Gaudium et Spes, Luctus et Angor . . ." 94

16: The Right Distance 101

Conclusion: "I Came to Cast Fire" 114

Glossary 120

Itineraries for Further Reading 133

Girard's Works in English 136

Index 139

Foreword

LUKE BURGIS

"A book must be the axe for the frozen sea inside us," wrote Franz Kafka.[1] An axe splits apart, but a fire transforms. Fire melts the ice of the frozen sea, and it clears a forest for new growth. Some books might be axes, but this one works differently: it is filled with the same fire that has been driving a two-thousand-year evangelical subversion of the old sacred forms to clear the way for something new.

This tension between old and new is at the heart of both René Girard's work and Fr. Elias Carr's introduction to Girard. I felt a sense of urgency reading *I Came to Cast Fire*, much like I did when I read Girard's work for the first time. The words quicken a fire within me, even as the world threatens to snuff it out. The hopeful message of this book, and the hopeful message at the core of Girard's work, is that this fire cannot be extinguished for those who are committed to battling to the end.

"What if triumph were not the most important thing? What if the battle were worth more than the victory?" asked René Girard in his last book, *Battling to the End*.[2] This book continues in that same spirit with an incisive view of history that sees Christ as its Lord as well as its redeemer. To battle to the end means to consciously and continually overcome the passivity that leads to death

---

1. Franz Kafka, *Letters to Friends, Family and Editors*, trans. Richard and Clara Winston (New York: Schocken, 1977), 16.

2. René Girard, *Battling to the End: Conversations with Benoît Chantre*, trans. Mary Baker (East Lansing, MI: Michigan State University Press, 2010), xvii.

and to choose instead the active love that leads to life. The fullness of that love is available in Christ.

And yet we so often hesitate at the invitation of divine love. We feel torn by a twofold movement of colonization, as Fr. Elias describes in these pages. We feel that we have been colonized by others' ideas and desires, and by a hostile culture and the many demands it imposes on us. And yet we are reminded constantly about the sins of the past, including our own. They are heaped upon our heads like burning coals. We confront those times when we have been the colonizers—when we have imposed our will on those we falsely view as enemies or threats to our autonomy.

On a human level, there is no way out of the cycles of reciprocal violence, shame, guilt, and cover-up that characterize the life of the world cut off from God. But Christ has given us an advocate, the Paraclete, whose fire destroys the old world and its fears, born of sin, and renews us with the same energizing power that the Apostles received on Pentecost—one that allowed them to boldly go to the ends of the earth, and even to their own deaths, proclaiming the Gospel.

Liberation is only possible through the power of the Holy Spirit, which is stronger than the powers that held the old world together. Freedom comes through the conversion that the Spirit makes possible.

Despite the many attempts to downplay or divorce Girard's ideas from the lived experience of Christianity, I don't believe mimetic theory can ever be fully understood except from within a life of faith. Girard, reflecting on his conversion experience later in life, said, "I'm convinced that God sends human beings a lot of signs that have no objective existence whatsoever for the wise and the learned. The ones those signs don't concern regard them as imaginary, but those for whom they are intended can't be mistaken, because they're living the experience from within."[3]

We may admire the stained-glass windows of a cathedral from the outside, but we see their resplendence and understand their true meaning only from the inside. Likewise, Girard's work is profoundly spiritual, as Fr. Elias' book makes clear—and that can be most fully appreciated as one attempts to live out the Gospel. The spiritual life is a journey of desire, a *via desiderii*, and Girard helps us understand the terrain, temptations, and obstacles along the way. His work is currently undervalued in spiritual theology. This book makes an important contribution.

Conversion of our desire entails setting fire to the merely familiar to make way for what is true, which may appear to us as new (or, in the words of St. Augustine, "so ancient and so new"[4]). The old world is passing away, and it's natural to want to cling to it. We're nostalgic for the old world because it's comfortable there. We can see cause and effect, and we can control things—sometimes through the violence, the scapegoat mechanism, which Girard warns us is part of the old sacred order.

Or perhaps we're nostalgic for the old world because we are ashamed of what we now know. Like Adam and Eve in paradise, we want to hide ourselves—sometimes even from God. Greek Orthodox theologian Timothy G. Patitsas speculates that perhaps Adam hid himself because the knowledge he gained from eating the forbidden fruit allowed him to see Christ on the cross, the Lamb that was slain since the foundation of the world, and this knowledge was simply too much for him to bear.

Whether we accept that interpretation or not, it amplifies the message of Scripture and history: confrontation with the truth is difficult, and is not even fully possible except in the light

---

3. René Girard, *When These Things Begin: Conversations with Michel Treguer*, trans. Trevor Cribben Merrill (East Lansing, MI: Michigan State University Press, 2014), 131–132.

4. Augustine, *Confessions*, trans. Frank Sheed (Park Ridge, IL: Word on Fire Classics, 2017), 258.

of Christ, who shows us the extent to which humanity deceives itself about who is a victim and who are the victimizers. "You will see the success of my theories when you recognize yourself as a persecutor," Girard once told a skeptic at a conference.[5] That is a truth that each of us must come to terms with.

There are now many books about Girard, but few that aim to speak to the heart as much as the head. This book is one of those few. We recognize our dependence on grace not by thinking about it hard enough, but through humility and love.

Girard believed that we are now living during the apocalypse, but his understanding of the apocalypse was very different from the image in the popular imagination, much of which has been shaped by bad movies. The apocalypse is not God's wrath destroying the world; that, Girard believed, was one of the many lies we tell ourselves to avoid coming to terms with the truth. The apocalypse, rather, is the final culmination in the great unveiling of who God is and who we are.

The great truth hidden since the foundation of the world—more foundational than the violence that has characterized so much of human history—is the divine love that created the universe and sustains it. That love has been made flesh and has come to cast fire. Fr. Elias has produced a book that is dangerous in the best sense of the word. If you read it well, you, too, may catch fire—and be made new.

---

5. Cynthia Haven, "Are We Ready to Listen to René Girard?," Zocalo Public Square, August 7, 2023, zocalopublicsquare.org.

Introduction

The Day I Discovered Girard

Let me tell you about the day that my life changed. In the summer of 2001, I was in my terrible twos as a baby priest at Holy Spirit Catholic Church in Annandale, Virginia. I had a gift certificate for the now-defunct Newman Book Store in Brookland near the Catholic University of America. A respected priest of the Archdiocese of Washington authored a pamphlet on Catholic literature in which he crisply characterized this store's wares as "some good"—hardly an endorsement. In the dank basement on Eighth Street, I browsed the shelves aimlessly, a pleasure that is increasingly lost in our online world. I rounded a corner, and the title *I See Satan Fall Like Lightning* and the author René Girard came into focus. His name was known to me because of a couple articles in *First Things* in which I experienced the first inklings of Girard's sweeping mimetic theory.

In broad brush strokes, Girard formulated his theory in three stages: mimesis, scapegoating, Christ. First, through his reading of novels, he discerned that human desires are mimetic or imitative of another's desire, and that these mimetic desires give rise to rivalries. Second, these accumulating rivalries threaten to destroy the community unless a scapegoat presents itself. When it does, the community blames the scapegoat for its crisis. Girard describes this sequence of events as the "scapegoat mechanism," by which the community is reborn through the expulsion of the victim. Ritual sacrifice, myth, and prohibitions sustain the new culture, which restrains mimetic rivalry. Girard speaks of persons or institutions that restrain violence, such as government, as the *katéchon* (the term is from St. Paul's Second Letter to the Thessalonians). Third, Girard argues that the violent origins of culture remained hidden until the Paschal Mystery revealed the scapegoat mechanism. Thereafter, the Holy Spirit, the Paraclete, operates in history, proclaiming the innocence of the scapegoat, which gradually undermines the *katéchon*. Today, the modern concern for the victim has become the one universal ethic that has created the first planetary culture. Yet we are in a perilous situation because mimetic rivalries are multiplying and intensifying rapidly. Without resorting to the scapegoat mechanism, humanity faces a decision: self-destruction or conversion.

As I read *I See Satan Fall Like Lightning* that summer, my head spun, my heart raced, and my imagination soared, because Girard's thought solved a problem for which I was not even aware that I was seeking an answer—namely, the difference faith must make in the world. If the faith is only an idea and never incarnated in our personal and social choices, then it is not Christian. Mimetic theory gave me a powerful way to interpret the signs of the times in the following year when both the events of September 11 and the clerical abuse scandals unfolded.

But mimetic theory is also very practical. I'll give you an example: As the headmaster of an elementary school, I needed to introduce a "fair share" policy for the parents' association because of the "free rider problem." Too many parents weren't doing their fair share. Those who were happy with the situation were unhappy with the new policy. I called a public meeting to explain the rationale for the policy, and easily over one hundred people came to the parish hall. After my presentation, one of the leading critics was raring to go at me. I stopped him, invited him up to the podium, and sat down among the audience. His tirade ignited resistance from other parents. I sat there and thought,

INTRODUCTION

Thank God others are speaking up. If I were up there, I would *feel* like everyone was against me because the critic would be among the audience. It would be all of them against me—polarization. Mimetic theory taught me that how one stages a meeting influences the likelihood of conflict. That meeting ended well. With the exception of a few parents, most agreed that the policy was indeed fair.

But not everyone feels that way. Commenting on mimetic theory, Catholic University of America professor Michael Pakaluk argues that "the theory is doubtful for many reasons."[1] Why? Since Pakaluk does not elaborate, one can only speculate. First, there is the sheer quantity of Girard's texts that makes coming to understand his thought time-consuming. Although his key insights can be listed easily, the evidence and argumentation that support them demand extensive knowledge of a variety of disciplines. Second, Girard developed his theory over decades, refining and altering his theory in the light of criticism and new data. Thus, one must have an overview of his entire corpus and cannot simply rely on reading a few of his works. Third, Girard makes claims that are more heuristic than theoretical; that is, he proposes many routes for further investigation as implications of his theory that are yet to be confirmed. Fourth, Girard's style of writing varies from scientific and literary to rhetorical or even homiletic. Consequently, his corpus is better considered from the perspective of the whole so as to nuance its parts. Fifth, simplifications of his thought sometimes miss key elements of his argument. These contribute needless misunderstandings, which Girard himself acknowledges.[2]

In this book, I am seeking to alleviate these "many reasons" to doubt Girard's theory through a careful and concise summary of

---

[1]. Michael Pakaluk, "The Immaculate Conception and Mimetic Desire," The Catholic Thing, December 8, 2020, https://www.thecatholicthing.org/2020/12/08/the-immaculate-conception-and-mimetic-desire/.

[2]. René Girard, *Evolution and Conversion: Dialogues on the Origins of Culture* (London: Bloomsbury Academic, 2017), 160.

mimetic theory over his entire corpus in light of its mature presentation. I have tried to write short, digestible chapters for those new to Girard, first by looking at Girard's life (chapter 1), then at the basic components of Girard's mimetic theory (chapters 2–8), and finally at how Girard sees these components playing out through human history (chapters 9–16). I have test-driven the text with those interested in, but unfamiliar with, mimetic theory. Any shortcomings in these simplifications lie with the author. The appendix contains a glossary of terms, itineraries for further reading, and a selected biography. Reading Girard is the best way to avoid misunderstandings, but it takes disciplined attention and reflection. One can also further benefit from participating in a community of readers to share and test one's discoveries. Mimetic theory's future is bright because there are still many paths to explore; I will describe one briefly in the conclusion. I hope that you will find this book a stimulating and amusing text that is merely your first step in coming to this man who has changed so many people's lives. As one plunges more deeply into his texts, one finds applications to everyday life and to global events to set the world on fire with the love of God.

CHAPTER I

Meet René Noël Théophile Girard

If the Roman playwright Plautus is correct when he states that a name is a prophecy (*nomen est omen*), then Girard's name overflows with meaning: René (*renatus*, "reborn"), Noël ("the birthday of the Lord," from *natalis dies Domini*), and Théophile (*Theophilus* [Θεόφιλε], meaning "lover of God"). Girard's life bears testimony to the enduring power of baptismal grace (René) that only needs to be stirred into flame to make one a lover of God (Théophile), who ceaselessly contemplates the mystery of Bethlehem (Noël). Like St. Luke the Evangelist, Girard "decided, after investigating everything carefully from the very first, to write an orderly account for you" (Luke 1:3). Girard's life project can be understood as his attempt—tentative and at times even intemperate—to offer a fresh account of the meaning of Christ, who "is the same yesterday and today and forever" (Heb. 13:8).[1]

Just five years after World War I, on the evening of Christmas day in 1923, Girard was born to an anticlerical, Jesuit-educated father, Joseph Frédéric Marie Girard (1881–1962), and a Catholic mother, Marie-Thérèse de Loye Fabre (1893–1967), in Avignon, France,[2] as

---

1. This short biography, based on Girard's Stanford University colleague Cynthia Haven's *Evolution of Desire*, provides context to the origins and development of mimetic theory. Feel free to read it later, if you want to jump into mimetic theory itself.

2. For centuries, the French kings coveted the papal enclave, which consisted of the Comtat Venaissin (acquired in 1274) and Avignon (acquired in 1348). Seven popes (1305–1378) and two antipopes (1378–1403) reigned in Avignon. In 1791, a plebiscite was held that became

the second of five children. His parents were well educated: his father was an *archiviste-paléographe*, a specialist in medieval studies, and a curator at the Palais des Papes (Palace of the Popes). His mother was the first woman of the region to earn a *baccalauréat* (secondary school degree). To appreciate this achievement, one should take note that in 1931, only 2.5 percent of the French population held this distinction.[3] By the age of thirteen, Girard ceased practicing his faith, even if he did not reject it: "I was raised in the double religion of Dreyfusism and Catholicism (on my mother's side), although I didn't learn about Péguy until much later."[4]

The blitzkrieg, the collapse of the Third Republic, and the inauguration of the Vichy government over non-German-occupied France overshadowed Girard's late teenage years. After completing a second baccalaureate with distinction in 1941, he weighed his options, deciding to spend another year at home to prepare for the entrance exam for his father's alma mater, the École Nationale des Chartes (National School of Chartres), a hotbed of Dreyfusard activism during his father's studies. The Écoles supported a larger intellectual project to shape French national identity.[5]

Studying in Nazi-occupied Paris for two years and then in liberated Paris for two more (1943–1947) left Girard underwhelmed.

---

the pretext for its annexation to France, which the papacy reluctantly recognized at the Congress of Vienna in 1815.

3. Cynthia Haven, *Evolution of Desire: A Life of René Girard* (East Lansing, MI: Michigan State University Press, 2018), 13.

4. Haven, *Evolution of Desire*, 15. The Dreyfus family was among those who moved to France after the newly organized German Empire (Kaiserreich) annexed Alsace and Lorraine (previously incorporated under French kings over the course of three centuries) in 1871. In 1894, Captain Alfred Dreyfus, a graduate of the elite École polytechnique (Engineering School) in 1878 and the highest-ranking Jew in the French army, was accused of sharing secrets with the Germans. Traditional anti-Jewish prejudices disposed the French to see Dreyfus as an alien outsider. Despite his protests of innocence and ambivalent evidence, the court of law and public opinion convicted him of treason and banished him to the penal colony on Devil's Island off of French Guiana. A small minority of critics, however, vociferously contested the unjust verdict until it was overturned in 1906. Among those who noted the parallel between this case and the Gospels was Charles Péguy, who fought as a Catholic and socialist to vindicate Dreyfus.

5. Through the scientific study of the vast number of mostly medieval documents pilfered from libraries, archives, and churches during the revolutionary period, the École trained professional librarians and archivists, who provided fodder for historians to control the present by interpreting the past according to the norms of positivism. See Haven, *Evolution of Desire*, 34.

"This was the worst experience of my life," he recalled. "I hated it. I hated Paris. I hated Paris more than any other city."[6] The southerner from Avignon on the margins of cosmopolitan Paris longed for home. Yet Girard observed that were it not for the Nazi occupation and the difficulty with travel, he might have abandoned his studies due to his nostalgia. Midway through his studies and immediately after the liberation of Paris, Girard witnessed retaliation against those who were perceived to be German collaborators, whether politicians or simply women who were accused of sleeping with the enemy.[7]

Girard's decision to go to America changed everything.[8] He had only expected to stay for two years; however, during his studies at Indiana University, he met his future wife, Martha McCullough, in 1948. Even though he struggled to gain a command of English—almost all his major texts he composed in French, which he spoke with a beautiful Provençal accent[9]—he had found a new home. In 1950, he earned his doctorate in history with a dissertation on the "American Opinion of France, 1940–1943." McCullough and Girard married at the local Methodist church on June 18, 1951, the day of his graduation.

Eventually, they would have three children: two sons, Martin and Daniel, and a daughter, Mary. Noting that Girard's career would never have been possible had he stayed in France, Benoît Chantre, with whom Girard published his last major work, *Battling to the End*, contends, "Girard is, like Tocqueville, a great *French* thinker—and a great *French* moralist—who could yet nowhere else exist but in *the United States*."[10] Girard's academic career did not take off quickly. Indiana let him

---

6. Haven, 28.
7. Haven, 36–39.
8. Haven, 49.
9. Jean-Pierre Dupuy, "A Tribute to René Girard," *Anthropoetics* 21, no. 2 (Spring 2016): anthropoetics.ucla.edu.
10. Haven, *Evolution of Desire*, 61. Emphasis in the original.

go because he did not publish sufficiently. He moved to Duke University and then Bryn Mawr College.

In late autumn of 1958, as he was working on the conclusion of his upcoming book, *Deceit, Desire, and the Novel*, Girard was increasingly preoccupied with the similarities between religious experience and the writings of certain novelists, who were brave enough to admit that our desires are not our own, but rather come from a model. This he would call mimetic desire. He moreover began to feel his own skeptical convictions coming under cross-examination. This wrestling first came to an intellectual climax: "Everything was there at the beginning, all together. That's why I don't have any doubts. There's no 'Girardian system.' I'm teasing out a single, extremely dense insight."[11] Girard's intellectual conversion consisted of a moment of insight that he spent the rest of his life exploring.

His spiritual conversion began shortly thereafter when Girard, while commuting on a train from Bryn Mawr to Johns Hopkins, where he was teaching, discovered a lesion on his forehead. The subsequent medical examination left open whether it was cancerous. Though it turned out to be of little consequence health-wise, it catalyzed his spiritual awakening and a return to his Catholic roots. In the ensuing weeks, Girard devoted himself, as never before, to taking Lent seriously. On Spy Wednesday, March 25, 1959, he received the good news that he was cancer-free.[12] (March 25 marks liturgically the Solemnity of the Annunciation, the joyful mystery of the Incarnation of the Lord, nine months before his birth, Christmas, when the Blessed Virgin granted her *fiat*, "Let it be done," to God's plan for salvation.) Through this near encounter with death, Girard underwent a paschal experience.

---

11. Haven, 112.

12. Haven corrects the somewhat confusing text from *When These Things Begin*, 131. There, Ash Wednesday is confused with Spy Wednesday, the day before the Triduum on which is recalled Judas' scheming to hand over Jesus to the authorities. The context makes it clear that Girard means the Wednesday of Holy Week. See Haven, *Evolution of Desire*, 118.

The moral conversion followed immediately thereafter. He found a priest to bless his marriage, allowed his sons to be baptized—his daughter would be born the following year—and committed himself to the practice of the Catholic faith. In retrospect, Girard's biographer Cynthia L. Haven writes, "The consent of the will occurred in what he [Girard] called the 'first conversion' experience. The second conversion gave him urgency, depth, and the endurance to take the next steps in the journey."[13]

While employed as a professor at Johns Hopkins University, Girard published the text that had contributed to his conversion, *Mensonge romantique et vérité romanesque*, in France in 1961. The title hinted at Girard's intellectual conversion. Literally rendered in English as "Romantic Lies and Novelistic Truth," it was later translated as *Deceit, Desire, and the Novel* and published in English in 1966. The title plays on the French word for novel (*roman*) and the nineteenth-century philosophy of Romanticism, which celebrated creativity, genius, and originality, especially in the arts.

Girard proposed the first elements of mimetic theory in terms of the experience of conversion as death and resurrection. His title in French explains what is at stake: modernity is founded on the "Romantic lie" that human beings determine their desires autonomously and freely, and the novelistic truth contradicts this claim, stating that mimetic desire more powerfully influences desire than reason or will.[14] Girard prized those novelists who had the honesty to acknowledge the Romantic lie in the face of this novelistic truth. In Girard's view, this would entail a death and resurrection experience, the ego dying through the truth that it is held in bondage to mimesis, and rising with a new sense of humility because it

---

13. Haven, 118.

14. By choosing "Romantic," Girard does not mean to exclude the other source of the modern myth of individualism: the liberalism of Enlightenment thinkers. Both sustain this myth.

no longer fears the truth that one is not original, but rather like everyone else.

In October 1966, Girard organized an international conference on "The Languages of Criticism and the Sciences of Man," at which an obscure philosopher, Jacques Derrida, introduced deconstructionism to American academia. According to this literary theory, texts communicate not so much objective truth (something true always and everywhere), but rather subjective wordplay in which a text can be decoded to find its hidden, unexpected meanings (something that is true for you but not for me). Derrida became an intellectual superstar. While Girard appreciated Derrida's early essay on Plato and the *pharmakos*, he also perceived a great threat to scholarship since deconstructionism manifested a lack of faith in reality itself.[15] If reality is unknowable or unreachable and therefore everything is just wordplay and interpretation, then what is left of the search for truth? Girard could not sacrifice the search for truth because he was coming to recognize the one truth that the postmodern world did not and could not abandon: the concern for the victim.[16] With the rising tide of deconstructionism and an increasingly tense rivalry with Derrida, Girard decided that it was best to withdraw from Johns Hopkins, taking a position at the State University of New York at Buffalo in 1968.

Nevertheless, it was a time of prodigious activity, as Girard was transposing his mimetic insights from *Deceit, Desire, and the Novel* to anthropology, ethnology, myth, ritual, and religion. The French public widely acclaimed Girard for the fruit of these labors, *La violence et le sacré* (*Violence and the Sacred*), published in French in 1972. In this second book, Girard focused on sacrifice rather than mimesis. This might have seemed surprising, but even before Girard had published *Violence and the Sacred*, he

---

15. Haven, 143.
16. René Girard, *I See Satan Fall Like Lightning*, trans. James G. Williams (Maryknoll, NY: Orbis, 2001), 177–178.

was already at work on his next book, which would bring biblical revelation and Christianity into this orbit.

Growing restless, Girard was lured back to Johns Hopkins University, an institution of which he was always fond, with an appointment to the prestigious Richard A. Macksey Humanities Center in 1976.[17] The English translation of *La violence et le sacré*, *Violence and the Sacred*, appeared in 1977. The following year, *Des choses cachées depuis la fondation du monde* was published in France—published in English nine years later as *Things Hidden since the Foundation of the World*. While *Violence and the Sacred* applied mimetic theory to archaic religion, *Things Hidden* introduced biblical religion and its singular role in demythologizing myth and uncovering the origins of culture. *Things Hidden* records Girard's conversations with two colleagues on a wide variety of matters in which he revealed the extent to which the Gospel played a fundamental role in his thought, causing some to part ways with his theory and others to become more deeply attracted to it. Girard acknowledged his own inadequacy for the task: "I hold that truth is not an empty word, or a mere 'effect' as people say nowadays. I hold that everything capable of diverting us from madness and death, from now on, is inextricably linked to this truth. But I do not know how to speak about these matters. I can only approach texts and institutions, and relating them to one another seems to me to throw light in every direction."[18]

Finally, in 1981, he became the Andrew B. Hammond Professor of French Language, Literature, and Civilization at Stanford University, where he taught until his retirement in 1995. His important works from this period include *Le bouc émissaire* (1982; *The Scapegoat*, 1986), *La route antique des hommes pervers* (1985; *Job: The Victim of His People*, 1987), *A Theater of Envy: William Shakespeare* (1991), and *Quand ces choses commenceront* (1994;

---

17. Haven, *Evolution of Desire*, 187–188.
18. René Girard, *Things Hidden Since the Foundation of the World*, trans. Stephen Bann and Michael Metteer (Stanford, CA: Stanford University Press, 1987), 446.

When These Things Begin, 2014). *The Scapegoat* consists of studies of Old Testament stories and "persecution texts," which in his view stand midway between myth, which conceals scapegoating, and the Gospel, which reveals it openly. His complete exegesis of Job applies mimetic theory to its reflection on the problem of evil and the suffering of the innocent. With *A Theater of Envy: William Shakespeare*, which Girard wrote in his second language, English, he wanted to cast the Bard's text in a new light, which, as it turned out, most Shakespeare scholars found neither illuminating nor wanted, jealously protecting their well-guarded ground from a novice interloper.

In 1990, he cofounded with his friend, the Innsbruck theologian Raymund Schwager, SJ, the Colloquium on Violence and Religion. Girard's mimetic theology and Schwager's dramatic theology developed in tandem after Schwager's discovery of Girard in 1972. Their independent lines of research converged and enriched their respective projects, which took on an institutional expression in the Colloquium.

After his retirement, Girard published major works including *The Girard Reader* (1996), *Je vois Satan tomber comme l'éclair* (1999; *I See Satan Fall Like Lightning*, 2001), *Celui par qui la scandale arrive* (2001; *The One by Whom Scandal Comes*, 2014), *Les origines de la culture* (2004; *Evolution and Conversion*, 2008), and *Achever Clausewitz* (2007; *Battling to the End*, 2010). In this period, no book stands out as more important than *I See Satan Fall Like Lightning*, a bestseller in France but a quiet seller in America (which has been reprinted more than twenty times). Appearing in French at the end of the second millennium of Christianity, and in English during the momentous year of 2001, this book—with a helpful introduction by Syracuse University professor James Williams—is the best place to start with Girard's works.

On March 17, 2005, René Girard was elected as one of the forty *immortels* by the members of the *Académie*

Française. For his achievements, Girard's friend and colleague from Stanford University, Michel Serres, named him for the first time "the new Darwin of the human sciences."[19] Ten years later, on November 4, 2015, Girard died peacefully in his home in Stanford, California, at the age of ninety-one. His requiem was held at St. Thomas Aquinas Church in Palo Alto ten days later, just after the November 2015 terrorist attacks in Paris. A memorial service took place on February 15, 2016, at the Abbey of Saint-Germain-des-Prés in Paris. Based on the text of Joseph Haydn's *Seven Last Words of Christ* and evoking the revolution of the Resurrection, Serres eulogized, "From that day on, the new earth, virgin and mother, generates a new era where time, newly oriented, turns its back on death. Death no longer lies before our time, as our term, but flees, defeated, behind us."[20]

The Resurrection changes everything. Girard's life and writings offer a glimpse of the new world brought into being on Easter morning, which forges ahead, now nearly two millennia later. The next chapters seek to unravel his "single, extremely dense insight."

---

19. Haven, *Evolution of Desire*, 226.

20. Michel Serres, "Hommage à M. René Girard, en l'église Saint-Germain-des-Prés," Académie française, February 15, 2016, academie-francaise.fr.

CHAPTER 2

The Big Question

What makes human beings different from other forms of life? Thanks to advances in science, we appreciate more and more the complex and wonderful history of life in the universe. We can only speculate, at this point, about the likelihood of life on other planets based on our knowledge of the conditions that are necessary for life to arise, survive, and thrive. Our only example of life in the universe, however, remains the earth; the rest is science fiction. Our *Pale Blue Dot*—the title of the popular astronomer Carl Sagan's book—teems with life. With plants and animals, we share this "common home," as Pope Francis puts it in his encyclical *Laudato Si'*, and yet we are decisively different from the rest of them. How? What is distinctively human?

While answers abound, culture seems a good place to start because humans are the only ones who express themselves in culture. What is culture? While in common daily language we associate "culture" with the artifacts of civilization—language, literature, art, government, economics, and so forth—the term really comes from a most human act, *cult*, which means "worship." The act of worshiping creates culture, not the other way around. It also creates politics and religion. We try, mostly unsuccessfully, to distinguish religion, culture, and politics, but they are really the same thing. "Culture" derives from *cult* (worship). "Politics" comes from *polis* (πόλις), the Greek word that is commonly rendered as "city" but really refers to the citizens who constitute a worshiping community. "Religion" (*religio*) first referred to a set of rituals and symbols that expressed the identity of its society. Only later, in the Enlightenment, did religion come to mean what it does today: a worldview or a belief system, both of which are very distant from its original communal meaning.

How did worship arise? This question has occupied many serious thinkers from the beginning of human history. Human cultures tell myths about their origins that explain the divine, natural, and social worlds. These myths likewise explain the origins of practices such as ritual, sacrifice, and taboos. With the turn to scientific explanations for the origins of things, new theories arose, explaining worship in terms of its useful functions, such as promoting social peace and good order, rather than accepting myths at face value. Girard's proposal should be seen as a continuation of this line of explanation. At the same time, however, Girard does not exclude the possibility of—indeed, he even argues for—explanations that transcend rationalistic or atheistic accounts of religion.

For example, Karl Marx argued that culture and religion (and more broadly, ideas in general) are the products of the economic organization of a society (slavery, feudalism, capitalism, socialism, etc.). Marx argued that human communities pass through distinct stages of economic organization that would lead to a paradisal condition free from coercion. Religion was the "opium of the masses." (Consider the importance of opium as an escapist drug in the nineteenth century over which wars were fought between the British and Chinese Empires—because it provided relief from the misery of modernization.)

Marx and his associate Friedrich Engels were atheists. Although they rationalized their atheism with their theories, it seems that their atheism—as it does with many—comes from their revulsion to the evil, cruelty, and injustice they witnessed. If there was a God, let alone a good God, how could he let these things exist? If there is no God, what, if any, limits are there in one's quest to eradicate suffering, evil, and injustice from the world? What followed in the wake of their cry was the establishment of communist societies, some of which exist to this day, and cultural Marxism, which poisons much of the rest of the world with its extension of class struggle to new domains such as race, gender, and ethnicity. While the social ills they wished to alleviate were no doubt real, their therapies often ended up killing the patient.

By contrast, Girard argues that religion explains human origins. He proposes scenarios by which protohumans might have become human—that is, a culture-making animal. This transition from protohuman to human takes place through a coevolutionary process of biology and culture—that is, the reciprocal interaction between nature and culture. "Nature" refers to the world that we experience around us as given (which today seems to be shrinking), whereas "culture" refers to the world that we experience as something we collectively and individually have made. At times, the distinction can be blurry. For example, if people are forced to dwell on a floodplain because they cannot afford to live elsewhere, is a flood strictly a natural disaster, or the result of both nature (given) and culture (made by humans)?

To discover a universal pattern to reconstruct his scenario of humanization, Girard appeals to two kinds of evidence. First, he extensively consults written sources, especially myths. He supplements these with nonliterary sources from anthropology (the study of human origins) and its subdisciplines, archaeology (the study of material evidence) and ethnology (the comparative study of human groups). He also consults ethology (the study of animal behavior) to uncover whether behavioral patterns in animals might have been adapted to meet the requirements of *homo sapiens*. He places all this evidence within an evolutionary framework, which tries to explain how living beings adapt to their environment to survive and thrive. Considering the evidence, Girard concludes that humanity is a child of religion, which emerges from the scapegoat mechanism. Put simply for the moment, the scapegoat mechanism provided a solution to the problem of unbounded violence that arose from humanity's mimetic (imitative) desire. This was not something devised by human ingenuity or reason; rather, the first human beings stumbled into it. Since ethologists have found evidence of such behavior in primates, perhaps it has prehuman antecedents. Whatever the case, the scapegoat mechanism and its consequences, ritual and religion, protected the young species from unlimited violence, the unintended byproduct of mimesis (imitation).

CHAPTER 3

Mimetic Desire: That Which Is Truly Ours

The next two chapters summarize the first key insight of Girard—namely, that human desire is mimetic in nature. This will be difficult to accept. Indeed, there will be a part of you that will surely resist this claim because it offends our everyday notion of ourselves as independent, self-governing individuals. First, I will explain mimetic desire and, in the next chapter, the Romantic lie—that is, the myth of modern individualism. Recall that Girard's intellectual conversion came as a result of this discovery. It was also hard for him, as it was for the novelists from whom he learned about mimetic desire, to accept at the start that our desires—what we most cherish as our very own—come from others. But seeking the truth entails the acceptance of difficult, even undesirable, conclusions. The truth is that we are not nearly as original or self-governing as we like to believe. Yet, with this knowledge, we can become more so. That is the paradox and the joy of Girard's discovery of mimetic desires. Let's begin.

THE METAPHYSICS OF MIMETIC DESIRE

Girard identifies mimetic desire as the essential difference between man and other animals. Though constrained by the same biological needs for food, shelter, reproduction, etc., the genetic determination of behavior (instincts, hierarchies of dominance, etc.) diminished during human evolution and opened the way for behavior based on wants (*désirs*) as well as needs (*appétits*). While needs are grounded in biology, wants are influenced strongly by other people who model desires; hence, we imitate and adopt their desires (mimetic). Indeed, because wants and needs blend, the role of the model affects both wants and needs. In either case, however, what is desirable in the other is not ultimately any particular thing—whether it be a person, relationship, object, experience, or feeling—but *being* itself. Or as Girard puts it himself, "All desire is a desire for being."[1] This requires some explanation.

When I was a kid shopping in the mall for clothing, I would go to the Gap. I saw the models wearing clothing that projected health, strength, and beauty. I wanted those clothes because I wanted to be that way. I wanted to *be* robust, strong, and attractive. However, after I bought the clothing and brought it home, I didn't look that way. I had confused the shirt with what was underneath—namely, the muscular physique of the mannequin. Instead of strong and handsome, I was dumpy or, as it was sometimes said, "husky." The clothing caught my attention, but what I really wanted was what was underneath. The "underneath" is being. I wanted to be someone else who was in shape, athletic, attractive. In mimetic theory, Girard sees that behind desires for success, wealth, status, pleasure, relationships, goodness, even love, is the longing for *being*, a longing to be more than what one currently is. Here, at the heart of Girard's naturalistic explanation of human beings, we find, perhaps surprisingly, a metaphysical category that points to our creaturely dependence on the Creator, who *is* Being itself.

Let's break this down. St. Thomas Aquinas argues we find a distinction in each thing between its nature (i.e., *what* something

---

1. René Girard, *When These Things Begin: Conversations with Michel Treguer*, trans. Trevor Cribben Merrill (East Lansing, MI: Michigan State University Press, 2014), 12.

is; an "essence" or *essentia*) and its existence (i.e., *that* something is; "being" or *esse*). So, while there is a multiplicity of expressions of being human (every person is unique), we are all nevertheless human. We all have the same nature. We're all, in a way, the same thing. But while we all possess a human nature (*what* we are), we do not possess the power to make ourselves exist (*that* we are). We simply experience our being here; we did not cause it. It is just something that is for us, and likewise for everything else in the universe. Since we do not make ourselves exist, we may conclude with philosophers that we must depend on a source—whose essence *is* its existence—for our own existence. This source is, in Aristotle's language, the first cause.

The Bible further clarifies this source of our existence: he has revealed himself as "I Am Who I Am" to the prophet Moses (Exod. 3:14), whose name we routinely encounter in the Bible under the title "Lord."[2] Human beings as creatures are thus contingent beings. We don't have to exist. But we are not an accident either—the product of laws and luck. We can see ourselves as beings loved into existence by Love itself. Someone wants us to be here.

We should also note at this point that human beings have two kinds of existence. Our bodily or physical (*physis* means body, among other things, in Greek) existence includes not only our body as such but also our emotions and our mental capacities that rely on our brain. Bodily existence is not only material but also, due to our mind, extends into the realm of ideas, abstraction, and contemplation. It is for this reason that we can marvel at the fact that our bodies share in the amazing history of the universe. Thanks to our souls, however, we also transcend our bodily existence as *meta*physical, "beyond-the-bodily," beings.

---

2. In light of a modern tendency to use the vocalized Hebrew name for God in songs (e.g., "Yahweh, I know you are near") and biblical translations, the Congregation for Divine Worship and the Discipline of the Sacraments, under the direction of Pope Benedict, directed the bishops to return to this venerable tradition of reverence for the transcendence of God and the holiness of his name. See "Letter to the Bishops' Conferences on 'The Name of God,'" June 29, 2008, usccb.org.

We are both. Pope St. John Paul II puts it this way: "Created in the image of God, man is both a corporeal and spiritual being. Bound to the external world, he also transcends it. Besides being a bodily creature, as a spirit he is a person. This truth about man is an object of our faith, as it is a biblical truth about his being constituted in 'image and likeness' of God."[3]

This understanding of human beings is theological in origin because God reveals it to us in Scripture. As corporeal beings, we depend on the air we breathe, the food we eat, the water we drink, the parents who made us, the families who raised us, the friends who rejoice in us, and the communities that sustain us. All of these corporeal dependencies become clear in the light of our spiritual dimension because all depend on God for their very existence.

Another metaphysical way of understanding our dependence relates to the discussion of potency and act. All created beings (everything and everyone but God) exist in the tension between *potency* (their capacity to become what they are according to their essence/nature) and *act* (reaching the fullness or perfection of their essence). We possess both at the same time, naturally, because this is according to our nature. Let me explain. I don't just become human when I am an adult (although some cultures have acted this way, treating children or the unborn as disposable). Rather, I am human from the moment of conception. Yet at the same time, it is also quite clear that our humanity is yet to be fully actualized because we are only a zygote.

---

3. John Paul II, "Man Is a Spiritual and Corporeal Being," general audience, April 16, 1986, in *Audiences of Pope John Paul II* (Vatican City: Libreria Editrice Vaticana).

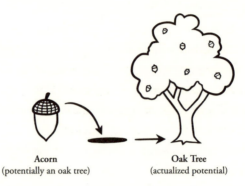

Acorn
(potentially an oak tree)

Oak Tree
(actualized potential)

But whether an acorn or a tree, it is always an oak.

It would also be false to imagine that we achieve the perfect state of our humanity before death. This cannot be the case. Before death our life is still tentative and its ultimate meaning obscure. As long as we live, we can frustrate our natural end by refusing to go along with it (that's sin). God has decided, however, to give the last word not to sin, but rather to the Word made flesh, Jesus, in whom there is always hope to get back on the right path (faith and Baptism). Only after death and judgment will the meaning of our life become definitive in terms of attaining through God's grace our nature or mature end. Put succinctly, we will live in the right relationship with God (knowing him face to face), our body (resurrection), our neighbor (the heavenly Jerusalem), and all the universe (the new creation). This and nothing else is the mature and perfect form of human nature.

To sum up, all being relies on God, who is pure existence (it is his nature to exist), dependent on nothing and no one, unlike everyone and everything else. Girard's claim about human desire, therefore, presumes a metaphysical understanding of being and becoming. Although that shirt from the Gap would never make me abundant in being through the attributes of strength and beauty, the resurrection of the body will.

A MIMETIC VOCATION

I can see now in hindsight the role that mimesis played in my vocation. When I say this, it is not meant in any way to discredit grace or God's call, but rather to perceive the way in which God works in our lives and how mimesis can be very positive. When I arrived at graduate school at the Catholic University of America (CUA) in 1990, I had no intention of becoming a priest. I had occasionally thought about it when I was growing up, but I did not know anyone who became a priest or was becoming one. We had none in our family. I went to public schools before university. We belonged to a large, post–Vatican II suburban parish where we had little contact with the clergy. I was never an altar boy. We often bounced around to different parishes for Sunday Mass, depending on how it fit into the schedule for televised sports. I simply lacked models.

That changed when I came to CUA. For the first time in my life, I felt like the world was right. I don't mean that everything was perfect there. I mean that as a Catholic child, I always felt out of place in public school, but I did not know why. My parents figured that everyone was Irish, Italian, or Jewish, just like back in New York City, so how different could public school really be? As I child, I could not articulate this sense of being out of place. It only became clear to me later, at CUA, where things made sense.

I met my first model—today he is a fellow canon of Stift Klosterneuburg, a more-than-nine-hundred-year-old abbey of Canons Regular of Saint Augustine who serve in Austria, Norway, and the United States—who in those days was not yet even a seminarian. I went to Mass with my parents at the Basilica of the National Shrine of the Immaculate Conception. At the end of the Saturday evening Mass on September 1, 1990, Stephen Nash (later Fr. Daniel) invited the students to be altar servers or lectors. My mom leaned over and said, "I bet you would like to do that." It was my Cana moment. She gave me the right nudge to do what

I already wanted to do but would have been afraid to do because I would have revealed my desire. She gave me the cover to do it, and I did it. I introduced myself and said I wanted to be a lector. He responded that they didn't need lectors, but servers. I said, "I've never served." He said, "You will learn." And I did. Over the following years, thanks to his example and his words, I learned to love the liturgy and the Catholic faith as he did. He took a kid from Long Island—as he was himself—and opened the world to me. His joy for life and love for people showed me that a priestly vocation embraces the world in all its joy and sorrow, in its adventures and mysteries.

After completing my master's degree, I decided to take a break and discern my vocation. I was weighing it over those two years. I went to Germany. It was a lonely experience much of the time, but the introspection and suffering did me good. I realized that the path that I was on in my studies was not the right one. It was time for a change. I moved to Virginia to live with my brother and a friend of his. It was a simple existence of work and prayer. In Lent of 1993, he and I mimetically inspired each other to pray the Rosary daily (I made it up as best as I could because I had not learned it as a child) and to read the New Testament. Whenever our desire wavered, we only needed to ask, "What page are you on?" and the desire to beat the other came back. By Easter we had not only finished the New Testament but made it into the Old Testament, only to hit the wall when we got to Leviticus.

During that spring, we joined a small, young adult–led Rosary and discussion group. On one occasion, a couple of the recently ordained priests came over to join us. One of them in particular struck me with his intelligent, attractive, and affable personality. I said to myself, *I want to be like him.* Not too much later, while I was alone praying in our little apartment near Ballston, Virginia, I said yes to my vocation. Immediately and subsequently, a profound peace filled my soul that never left me despite all the turmoil and trials of the seminary.

During my time in formation, God blessed me with great role models, fathers who also later became brothers in the priesthood and friends: Monsignor Pereda, Monsignor McKay, and Fr. Aldo. Friends are amongst God's greatest graces because they are the models one can safely imitate. I learned so much from these men. If I am any good as a priest, it is largely thanks to their example and friendship. Finally, on May 15, 1999, I was ordained a priest. Fr. Daniel tells me that he has never seen anyone before or since who was so happy on his day of ordination.

MIMETIC DESIRE IN SLOW MOTION

To understand desire, one must distinguish between desire as a *capacity*, which is common to human beings, and desire as *what one wants*, which is open, mobile, and changeable. For example, I am hungry, but what do I want to eat? I am out at a French restaurant, and I order *foie gras* because everyone is, even though I hate liver, or so I thought. Or why don't I want the newest iPhone even though my colleagues have just gotten them? Why are some desires strong and others weak? What might account for these differences?

Girard suggests that people do not know *what* to desire because it is not a matter of knowing, but rather of wanting. Rarely arising from rational calculation or careful planning, desire often feels spontaneous and surprising. We cannot force ourselves to want such and such. It appears mysterious to us. We do not know why we want what we want, but we would like to find out.

Girard describes human desire as "mimetic" because he has observed a link between what people want and who else wants it. *Mimesis* is the Greek word that we know in English as "imitation" (from the Latin *imitatio*). Mimetic desire explains that what we desire often depends profoundly on what *others* desire. We adopt the desires of others, mostly without ever realizing it. This begins right away as an infant. Before we have the use of reason, we are schooled in mimetic desire. We observe others, and they help us to specify what we want. It is hardly surprising to see children imitating their parents or siblings. As we become adolescents, our peer groups and friends provide compelling models, as do teachers, coaches, and celebrities. By adulthood we may attain sufficient self-knowledge to become aware of our patterns of wanting, creating a significant place for planning and deliberation.

This is not to say, however, that all wanting is therefore only mimetic, but rather to claim that for human beings, other human beings do play a big role in what we want specifically. Why do I fall in love with this or that person? In part, because someone else has made this person lovable in our eyes. This gives rise to the bizarre love triangles of literature and daily life. In those situations, imitation is certainly not "the sincerest form of flattery" because of the threat of competition and loss. Indeed, since flattery can also be insincere and manipulative, this saying comes under further suspicion. Observing that the original feels cheapened by the copycat or the knockoff, Oscar Wilde elongated the phrase to "imitation is the sincerest form of flattery *that mediocrity can pay to greatness.*" Does anyone believe a "Folex" (fake Rolex) praises a Rolex? There is something deeply unsettling about imitation.

THE BENEFITS

As a universal capacity of being human, mimesis explains both cultural diversity and personal idiosyncrasy. Human beings as culture-making animals come in many expressions. Mimesis makes human behavior plastic, thereby increasing fitness for survival by an expanding scope of adaptive flexibility to respond successfully to environmental challenges. Indeed, it is likely that mimesis accelerated human evolution as it added a new environmental pressure on the brain to be able to manage exciting and dangerous possibilities.[4] Mimesis contributes to the transmission of culture. Children learn through imitation, acquiring language and other skills for social success. Learning their culture's ethos, they become part of the community and eventually model it to the next generation.

Mimetic desire also confers the capacity for openness to others, which can lead both to desiring the good for the other (*ti voglio bene*, "I want your good") and escaping from self-preoccupation.[5] At the same time, it can corrupt if we do not learn to resist those desires that are destructive to our neighbor and ourselves. Although mimetic desire seems mysterious and powerful, with the right formation, Girard strongly affirms that we are free to choose to imitate well, even in the presence of powerful temptations to succumb to conflicts. This education in desire requires both the discovery of mimetic desire and its consequences (rivalry, violence, scapegoating, and culture) as well as personal conversion.

Mimesis structures interpersonal relationships by linking desire and being.[6] Again, "all desire is a desire for being"; Haven adds, "And the being we long for becomes wrapped up in a person, who becomes idol, and eventually, rival, locked in an impossible conflict for an object, an honor, a promotion, a lover, or the esteem of others, which is in itself a shorthand for a bigger battle with bigger forces."[7] What we want most is to be. Since we begin in ignorance of this condition, we need enlightenment, which many religious, philosophical, and spiritual traditions seek to address. We can learn to perceive this fundamental desire for being if we become conscious of our metaphysical situation. But is knowledge enough? No, we

---

4. René Girard, *Things Hidden Since the Foundation of the World*, trans. Stephen Bann and Michael Metteer (Stanford, CA: Stanford University Press, 1987), 93–94.

5. René Girard, *The Girard Reader*, ed. James G. Williams (New York: Crossroad, 1996), 64.

6. Burton Mack, "Introduction: Religion and Ritual," in *Violent Origins*, ed. Robert G. Hamerton-Kelly (Stanford, CA: Stanford University Press, 1987), 13.

7. Cynthia L. Haven, *Evolution of Desire: A Life of René Girard* (East Lansing, MI: Michigan State University Press, 2018), 107.

need more than knowledge; we also need a model who can motivate us to desire well.

TRIANGULAR DESIRE

Although mimesis is triangular, consisting of (x) the subject (or person), (y) the model (or other/mediator), and (z) the object,[8] its geometry is not a triangle:

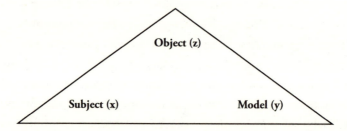

Rather, it is something more like a sequence, at least at the beginning. For the subject, the model conveys desirability on the object: I want the object because the model wants it.

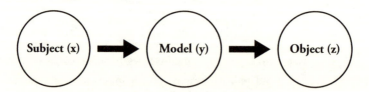

The subject refers to the person who desires that which the model possesses—namely, the object. To bring out different facets of the one whom one imitates, Girard uses three different terms: (1) the "model," (2) the "other," and (3) the "mediator."

The "model" generally proposes a desirable object to the subject unconsciously; the model is simply going about his or her business.

---

8. René Girard, *Deceit, Desire, and the Novel: Self and Other in Literary Structure*, trans. Yvonne Freccero (Baltimore, MD: Johns Hopkins University Press, 1966), 2–3.

Of course, those who understand this process can manipulate it for their advantage. In any case, no model is original in a metaphysical sense. Only God is the source of his own existence. The same goes for desires. We acquire them from others, and then we model them for others. This is a dynamic reality that is constantly happening. By the time we become aware of it—if we ever do—we have already been imitating and modeling desires for many years.

Let's take an example: the famous case in which Solomon adjudicates between two prostitutes claiming to be a child's mother (1 Kings 3:16–28). In terms of mimetic desire, the child is the object. One woman wants to be the other woman. In order to do so, she wants what the other has—namely, the child. Recall, the desirable object is not an end in itself. She doesn't really want the child. She wants to be the other woman. In order to become her, she wants what she has. Therefore, the conflict arises from the fact that the lying prostitute desires to be the honest prostitute. By possessing the child, she becomes more like the woman she desires to be. The child is not in itself important; he is a means to an end.

The honest prostitute willingly sacrifices her own desire to vindicate her claim as the child's true mother in order to protect her child from Solomon's threat to divide the child in two.

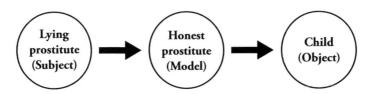

The lying prostitute, on the other hand, willingly allows the sacrifice of the child because in the end she truly wants what her model, the honest prostitute, has: she wants to be her. She perceives her as being more real, as more abundantly existing, than herself. She wants to be the honest prostitute because behind all desiring is the desire to be. The object, the child, loses its salience in the conflict and recedes in importance.[9]

The second term, the "other," simply places the two persons in opposition.

The third term, "mediator," refers to the role that the model or the other plays as one who mediates desire. "Mediation" has a number of important meanings for Girard to which we shall return below. In brief, in a mimetic relationship, both the subject and the model mediate desire to each other; Girard calls this "double mediation." "Internal mediation" and "external mediation" describe two kinds of distance between the subject and the model that indicate the likelihood of conflict. In the end, three terms—model, other, and mediator—refer to the same person, although the context might suggest the reason for choosing one term over the others.

The object is not the final point of desire. Beyond the object—whatever or whoever that might be—is desire's true aim: the model's being.[10] This metaphysical hunger causes the acquisitive nature of human desire. Poor in both being and desires, the subject seeks to appropriate the being of the other, the model, through imitating what the other desires, through adopting his words, deeds, and relationships, ultimately becoming the other. This is the basis for advertising and marketing, associating a good or service with an attractive model. Strange as it seems, we are radically dependent on God, creation, and others, yet our modern worldview tells us that we are independent as individuals and that we determine our desires.

9. René Girard with Pierpaolo Antonello and João Cezar de Castro Rocha, *Evolution and Conversion: Dialogues on the Origins of Culture* (London: Continuum, 2008), 153–154.
10. Girard, *Deceit, Desire, and the Novel*, 53.

CHAPTER 4

The Romantic Lie: "I Am an Original"

Under the influence of the Gospel, the West invented a concept of the self that gave rise to modern individualism, which places the rights of the individual over those of the community. It is the air we breathe; Girard, however, claims that this air is foul. Although there is much good in affirming the dignity of every human being and defending the freedom of each person to pursue life, liberty, and happiness, it is wrong when it is taken to the extreme. When individualism forgets our real dependence on each other, on our environment, and on God, it goes terribly and dangerously wrong because it is untethered from the truth. This Girard calls the "Romantic lie." Let's give an example of how this lie works so powerfully on us.

In *Wanting*, Luke Burgis recounts the chilling machinations of the American Tobacco Company to ignite a desire in American women to take up smoking, a hitherto unconventional behavior.[1] The company's president tapped Eddie Bernays, a nephew of Sigmund Freud and later theorist of public relations, to devise the strategy. He rebranded smoking cigarettes as "torches for liberty." Leaving nothing to chance, he chose the Easter Sunday parade in Manhattan on March 31, 1929 (just six months before the bubble

---

1. Luke Burgis, *Wanting: The Power of Mimetic Desire in Everyday Life* (New York: St. Martin's, 2021), 31–35.

burst in the stock market crash), to launch his campaign for women's liberation (and profit for the American Tobacco Company): "At the appointed time, following Bernays's instructions, the models whipped out their Lucky Strikes and smoked them in their flapper hats and fur-trimmed coats as they walked flouncily down the street."[2] The ploy tripled sales of Lucky Strikes. Its success rested on "the illusion of autonomy—because that's how people think desire works. Models are powerful when they are hidden. If you want to make someone passionate about something, they have to believe the desire is their own."[3]

Burgis underscores Girard's profound insight that desire is more intense when it dovetails with the illusion that it is mine—the Romantic lie. People want to believe that they are original, different, unique. Yet, the reality is that we all share the same metaphysical predicament—namely, that we are dependent on just about everything, from the air we breathe, to the water we drink, to the food we eat, to the language we speak, to the communities in which we live, to name but a few.

Indeed, our situation today is even more desperate. This metaphysical poverty has grown acute in modernity because of the myth of personal autonomy, which seduces everyone into believing that they already possess the resources to create themselves. The 1992 Supreme Court decision in *Planned Parenthood v. Casey*, authored for the majority by Justice Anthony Kennedy, captures this sentiment perfectly: "At the heart of liberty is the right to define one's own concept of existence, of meaning, of the universe, and of the mystery of human life."[4] Even if it were true that liberty is the right to define one's own existence, etc.—and this is highly contestable, as we have just seen, by the interdependence that characterizes human existence—are we able to do this?

2. Burgis, 34.
3. Burgis, 35.
4. Planned Parenthood of Southeastern Pennsylvania et al. v. Casey, Governor of Pennsylvania, et al., 505 U.S. 833, 851 (1992).

In Girard's view, this modern celebration of genius, difference, and originality, as expressed in Justice Kennedy's claim about liberty, is fraught because it puts an impossible burden on individuals by ignoring mimesis. Human beings in themselves cannot define their "own concept of existence, of meaning, of the universe, and of the mystery of human life," because they are neither autonomous nor self-sufficient, but always dependent on others for their oft mercurial desires. Asking one to base one's life on one's own resources—which are moreover always limited by any number of factors—is a recipe for chronic disappointment, second-guessing, inertia, anxiety, depression, despair, and worse. In this case, the better or the perfect always becomes the enemy of the good, and I obsess about the "fear of missing out" ("FOMO"), a social media–related anxiety disorder.[5]

Even the presumption that one can define one's own existence is structurally the same as everyone else. In other words, the more we assert our differences, our individuality—what is our very own—the more we are just like everyone else, and the more we become the same. When I was a teenager, I listened to WLIR, a radio station that invited their listeners to "dare to be different."[6] What a perfect scheme. Yes, by listening to this station, I would be different—i.e., better—from the rest, and with no further effort than tuning in. It only dawned on me later that alternative music—as it was sometimes called—often was nothing other than alternative marketing because those songs I liked often became popular just a few months later. I wasn't any different in the end. I was like everyone else.

---

5. Mayank Gupta and Aditya Sharma, "Fear of missing out: A brief overview of origin, theoretical underpinnings and relationship with mental health," *World Journal of Clinical Cases* 9, no. 19 (2021): 4881–4889.

6. There is even a 2017 documentary about the cultural significance of WLIR: *New Wave: Dare to be Different*.

CHAPTER 5

The Right and Wrong Distance: External and Internal Mediation

Mimetic desire is inherent in human relationships. Distance in a social rather than a spatial sense is the key variable in whether such mimetic desire will lead to peaceful imitation or violent conflict. Sufficient distance between individuals prevents the escalation to the extreme because it places the subject and model far enough apart to make conflict unlikely. Girard calls this "external mediation." Its opposite, "internal mediation," refers to too little distance, which makes rivalry likely.[1] Burgis explains this distinction amusingly by naming two domains: "Celebristan" consists of those people who are a great distance from us (celebrities, fictional characters, historical figures, and leaders) and "Freshmanistan" is populated by those who are close to us (colleagues, friends, acquaintances, and family members).[2]

A trip on Air Mimétique may help illustrate the point. Huddling around the gate awaiting our boarding, group one is called, then two, then three—and finally eight, our group. We make our way down the jetway and cross the threshold into Celebristan: the

---

1. René Girard, *Deceit, Desire, and the Novel: Self and Other in Literary Structure*, trans. Yvonne Freccero (Baltimore, MD: Johns Hopkins University Press, 1966), 9.
2. Luke Burgis, *Wanting: The Power of Mimetic Desire in Everyday Life* (New York: St. Martin's, 2021), 47.

exclusive suite of first class, with its luxurious and spacious seats. The already-seated, champagne-sipping occupants avert their eyes from the procession of neck pillows and carry-on bags that passes them by, marching to their doom. Crossing the last boundaries, we arrive at our center seats. The overhead bins are already full. We hunt for space elsewhere. Noticing the neighboring passengers have not yet arrived, a secret desire arises: perhaps they won't come at all, and we can stretch out. Then the fear follows: if they do come, we will be wedged into the middle. Our eyes dart around the cabin for empty seats. They finally arrive, and there are no empty seats. We resign ourselves to our fate. Sitting in the front of the cabin of Freshmanistan, we see the veil descend once the flight reaches altitude. The nearest bathroom is forward, but we must go backward, navigating legs and arms and shoulders down the narrow aisle.

As our flight on Air Mimétique demonstrates, Celebristan is literally within our sight but out of our reach. We have seen these beguiling, well-dressed, hale people (much like those whom one encounters on social media, at the movies, and in advertising). We admire them and their jet-set lifestyle, but somehow our paths never cross. They live in their world (whether it is behind the curtain, across vast lawns, or up high in a penthouse, or in a sordid, louche bar, on a seedy corner, or in deep and secluded Kentucky hollers—because mimesis works in surprising directions), and we live in ours.

The Celebristani, Burgis writes, are those "who mediate—or bring about changes in our desires—from somewhere *outside* of our social sphere, and with whom we have no immediate and direct possibility of competing on the same basis."[3] He identifies three kinds of safe distance: "They might be separated from us by time (because dead), space (because they live in a different country or aren't on social media), or social status (a billionaire, rock

---

3. Burgis, 47. Emphasis in the original.

star, or member of a privileged class)."[4] For these reasons, one can peacefully imitate them without fear of conflict. One watches the television show *Justified*, admires Raylan Givens, and thereby takes up bourbon drinking and cowboy hat wearing, and resolves to visit Harlan County, even though one cannot find Kentucky on the map. There is no chance of rivalry, unless of course one gains the attention of the distant model—like a small business that infringes on the trademarked brand of a large business. For example, in 2023, the Supreme Court ruled unanimously in favor of Jack Daniel's Tennessee Whiskey (not to be confused with Kentucky Bourbon) against a dog toy manufacturer's parody product.[5]

Throughout history, Celebristan was mostly inaccessible. Traditional societies set up firm barriers to prevent social mobility and therefore maintained external (safe) mediation. When the rulers were truly aristocratic—the rule of the excellent (from the Greek *areté*), which no doubt was a rarity—one could admire and imitate their virtues according to one's place in society (whether in a traditional aristocracy or the modernized version, a meritocracy). But when these barriers weaken, as they have with the arrival of modernity and increasing social mobility, or when one can live within any group, then external mediation succumbs to internal mediation. The greatest threat to a king, for instance, came often from his male relatives, who shared his social world.

With Freshmanistan, Burgis captures the anxieties and aspirations of new students in a high school (or college) or, later, at any job. One looks for a group within the group to create a livable situation. Group membership depends upon imitating one's models in fashion, speech, music, activities, and other preferences that shift from year to year, season to season. Yet while specific choices do change, once the choices are made, they are uniform for as long as they endure. For example, when annually hearing

4. Burgis, 49.
5. Jack Daniel's Properties, Inc. v. VIP Products LLC, 599 U.S. 140 (2023).

confessions in preparation for Confirmation, Fr. Gabriel, one of my confreres, noticed that the *confirmandi* seemed to all wear the same shoes: Uggs a few years ago, now vintage sneakers.

Of course, some freshmen might opt for models who are upperclassmen or, more distant still, faculty members (cue Doris Day singing "Teacher's Pet"). In any case, Freshmanistan is rife with rivalry and competition, with fears of imitators trying to steal what is mine (or ours).

When I was in junior high school—and there could be no better example of the hellish nature of Freshmanistan, even if it is a transient state closer to purgatory—I discovered that I liked The Who. Why? Who knows? I bought their record *Who Are You*, which is fine.[6] But then I publicly declared my belonging when I got a concert T-shirt from those days—the white center print with the short black arms. Much to the horror of other students to whose group I did not belong, I had appropriated their symbol. I was not the sort of student who should be wearing their stuff!

Even as Celebristan is beyond reach to those on the outside (external mediation), and therefore a safe distance, those inside (internal mediation) experience it as Freshmanistan, where the distance is too close. While no one expects the passengers in business to stage a revolution against those in first, their feelings of anxiety and insecurity about their respective positions and threats to their positions still characterize the Air Mimétique experience. And all of this, of course, works because Celebristan exists in the first place (external mediation) and those who dwell in their respective Freshmanistans (internal mediation) fear the legal and social consequences of violating the rules that structure these relationships. But what happens in a world where there is

---

6. Evidently, even the album's titular track has a mimetic background. After having earned a large royalty check, Pete Townshend went to a bar to salve his conscience. By chance he met Paul Cook and Steve Jones of the Sex Pistols, who looked up to The Who as pioneers for punk rock. Townsend felt deeply conflicted. Had his admirers known about the very large royalty check they got earlier that day, they would likely see him as a sellout. He thus fled the bar and promptly passed out, writing "Who Are You" the next day.

no Celebristan (for this did not always exist) and where the Fresmanistani have few or no constraints? When we ask this question, we are approaching the first stage of humanity, where there was no state, government, legal or judicial system, policing, incarceration—or even the rudiments of sacrifice, ritual, and prohibition.

While we all look longingly at the Celebristani, we always remain Freshmanistani. Our immediate lifeworld is always Freshmanistan. Even though our models are too close not to be competitors, we retain our freedom. But in some cases, that attraction is too strong. We are a dog with a bone, and we refuse to give up because others want that bone too. The competition intensifies.

CHAPTER 6

Mimetic Rivalry: When Desire Goes Wrong

Girard contends that mimetic desire is the source of humanity's singular status as beings who are free to learn and to love. Yet, a dangerous byproduct accompanies mimetic desire: unbounded intraspecies violence. While interspecies violence in the animal world in terms of prey and predator is the norm, intraspecies violence is not.

Even though ethology (the study of animal behavior) is a new discipline, its preliminary findings suggest that animals have genetically determined limitations on violence through networks of dominance, and even perhaps exhibit a pattern of behavior that could be a precursor to the scapegoat mechanism.[1] Thus, mimetic desire causes unbounded intraspecies violence, to which we turn in this chapter, and requires a solution: the scapegoat mechanism, to which we will turn in chapters 7 and 8.

MIMETIC RIVALRY: DOUBLE MEDIATION AND THE SCANDAL

Whenever a mediator—that is, the subject's model—senses the subject's interest in the object, this causes "double mediation."

---

1. Girard cites Konrad Lorenz's *On Aggression*, in which he describes an instinctual pattern of behavior by which conflicting geese polarize their aggression on a third object. See René Girard with Pierpaolo Antonello and João Cezar de Castro Rocha, *Evolution and Conversion: Dialogues on the Origins of Culture* (London: Continuum, 2008), 71–75.

Put simply, both now mediate desire to each other. The mediator or model's desire is inflamed because the subject now becomes a model for him. Driving, for example, easily becomes a mimetic rivalry of double mediation. When we detect that someone is trying to pass, suddenly there is a competition in which there are winners and losers. So you speed up. What does the other driver do? Who will win? Why are we competing? Driving is an intensely mimetic activity. A better understanding of this might make traffic engineering more successful, or perhaps we just have to wait for computer-driven cars, which do not succumb to mimetic desire.

Once the model realizes that the subject wants something, he reciprocates by wanting the object more. Interestingly, the now-desired object might have lost its desirability until that moment. This Girard sees in the classic love triangle depicted in novels, in which a loveless relationship is resuscitated through the desiring of another. Therefore, the subject and his model stoke each other's desire. They become obstacles to the realization of each other's desire. In this spiral of envy, the object's desirability diminishes, whereas the desire for the being of the other intensifies.[2] Indeed, the original object can often disappear for the moment because the subject and model are completely fixated on each other. They are entirely opposed, face to face.

Girard employs the biblical terms "scandal"/"scandalize" (*skandalon/skandalizein*) to describe the obstacles over which people stumble (the literal sense of "scandal" in Greek). In double mediation, both the subject and the model scandalize each other because they become the obstacles to reaching their desires. Scandals simultaneously fascinate and repulse, eliciting reciprocity and the escalation to the extremes.[3] The subject and the model growingly resemble each other, becoming doubles or twins. The

---

2. René Girard, *Deceit, Desire, and the Novel: Self and Other in Literary Structure*, trans. Yvonne Freccero (Baltimore, MD: Johns Hopkins University Press, 1966), 85.

3. René Girard, *I See Satan Fall Like Lightning*, trans. James G. Williams (Maryknoll, NY: Orbis, 2001), 16–18.

frequent appearance of enemy brothers or twins in myth (e.g., Romulus and Remus; Loki and Thor) exemplifies the phenomenon of doubles.[4] For those on the outside of the conflict, the two increasingly come to resemble each other because the rivalry eliminates differences. One need only think of two persons engaged in a brawl: everything that distinguishes them falls away under the weight of increasing violence.

From the inside, however, their loss of difference (which is another way of saying they are becoming identical) causes each to reassert ferociously the essential difference—namely, in this case, that the other is at fault because he is trying to steal what is mine.[5] Each claims the role of the aggrieved party, who is merely responding to the prior attack of the other. As Girard notes, human beings always believe that they are retaliating. As the injured party, the other is always the aggressor. Both claim to be responding, reacting, defending. Indeed, no one attacks; all merely defend.[6]

In double mediation, if there is no final resolution, the scandal oscillates from one extreme to the other: too near (one is tempted to dominate the model) to too distant (one is tempted to be dominated by the model).[7] One becomes the master or the servant. This situation is inherently unstable. Thus, in long-term mimetic rivalries, battles are fought, but the war continues. The winner temporarily restores the illusion of his autonomy, and the loser temporarily sees the other as greater, more sacred, and overflowing in being. The loser moreover seethes resentment, even as a new campaign is underway.

In August 1995, I met many of my fellow classmates at the Pontifical North American College. The Knights of Columbus

---

4. Girard, 22.

5. Girard, *Deceit, Desire, and the Novel*, 99–100.

6. René Girard, *Battling to the End: Conversations with Benoît Chantre*, trans. Mary Baker (East Lansing, MI: Michigan State University Press, 2010), 18.

7. Girard, 124.

had kindly arranged for a place for us to gather at JFK Airport because we were all arriving from different parts of the country to fly on Trans World Airlines to our new home in Rome. Seminarians for the North American College get a lot of mixed messages. We were told that we were not special or better. Okay, but if that were the case, why were we being sent to Rome? Many were academically inclined and ambitious to serve the Church, if not also themselves. In fact, six of us were profiled in the book *The New Men: Inside the Vatican's Elite School for American Priests*. (I was not one of them.)

The old men, as the other seminarians were called, warned us new men that many of us would spend our second year getting rid of the relationships we made in our first year. How right they were. As new arrivals in a strange land in a group of unknown people, it was easy to gravitate toward others on the flimsiest of grounds. There was a sort of desperation to find one's place, and there was a lot of jockeying for position. For example, as free weeks and holidays approached, one anxiously tried to find travel companions. One did not want to be left behind. What would the others think?

In my first year, I found myself in an involuntary friendship out of which I did not know how to gracefully bow. Such is the burden of youth. It was highly mimetic and stressful. I felt trapped. A solution arose unexpectedly. I went to bed one night, and the next day I woke up entirely unable to abide this person anymore. My entire being revolted against him. I cannot say what brought this about, but some part of me wanted to be set free from this entanglement in double mediation. The summer break soon arrived, and our paths diverged peacefully. Only once more did I undergo such a startling and sudden transformation. In both cases, it gave me the strength to put distance between the other and myself.

Double mediation does not exist in a vacuum, but rather in a social context where multiple conflicts rage. In most groups, factions and parties coalesce, subsuming interpersonal conflicts. Groups that were once at odds form alliances against their common enemies, leaving previous disagreements behind—at least for the moment. Girard calls the communal character of mimetic rivalry a "plague" or "social contagion."

PLAGUE / SOCIAL CONTAGION

The invisible spread of mimetic rivalry mirrors the invisible spread of a bacterial or viral contagion. When Girard speaks of premodern plagues as a mimetic crisis, as in Oedipus' Thebes, he is not denying the biological character of a plague, but rather emphasizing its equally social character. The recent pandemic made this clear. In the name of health and security, opposite conclusions were drawn. Each group accused the other of sacrificing someone: either the elderly, the immunocompromised, and the poor, or the young, the healthy, and the self-employed. It moreover called into question the boundaries between nature and culture, biology and politics, science and ideology. This blurring signifies a mimetic crisis when all differentiation between people collapses under the weight of the mimetic contagion. This lack of difference, which for Girard means that all become identical, announces the threat of imminent violence. The cycle of attraction and repulsion continues until a final resolution. The community, in danger of being consumed by its own mimetic contagion and destroying itself, discovers a way out: it collectively polarizes against a third party declared guilty for causing the crisis. This third party Girard calls "the scapegoat."

CHAPTER 7

The Scapegoat

In today's usage, the "scapegoat" is the one who is blamed or the sin-bearer. Perhaps we have felt that we have been blamed unfairly and played the scapegoat. It happens in families and workplaces, in classrooms and communities, in politics and the Church, nationally and globally. It happens wherever there are human beings. Scapegoating, as we will see, was not always something human beings understood. The change came with biblical religion, reaching its culmination in the Gospels. Thereafter, that cat was out of the bag. The truth about the innocence of the victim undermined people's confidence in determining the good guys and the bad guys. Today, much of this has been turned on its head, as those who were once thought to be good are regularly characterized as the source of all evil ("dead white men," as they used to say in my college days). Instead of vindicating the victims of injustice, we start new cycles of victimization.

Girard borrows the scapegoat from the rituals of the Day of Atonement, or Yom Kippur (Lev. 16). He sees the inclusion of this rite on Yom Kippur as incorporating a much older, pre-biblical tradition found in other cultures, such as ancient Greece. In the ritual, two goats are selected by lots: the first is sacrificed to the Lord as a sin offering, but the second has all the sins of Israel laid upon its head and is driven out from the community into the desolate place of Azazel. Languages influenced by the Bible and its Greek Septuagint and Latin Vulgate translations render the term differently. The Italian, *capro espiatorio*, follows the Greek, *tragos aperkhomenos*, the "expiating goat" or "atoning goat." (It is also worth noting that the term "tragedy" comes from *tragos*, "goat"). By contrast, the French, *bouc émissaire*, follows the Latin *caper emissarius*, which underscores the goat's role as a representative (emissary) of the community. The English version comes from the influential Protestant biblical scholar William Tyndale, who interpreted the Hebrew through the Latin to mean "the goat that departs"—the "(e)scape goat." Modern translations in English favor "goat for Azazel" as a more accurate reading of the Hebrew. Whatever the translation, the role of the goat remains the same: it is the sin-bearer, which expiates the sins of Israel by representing the community.

Scapegoating is so obvious today that it is nearly impossible for us to imagine a world in which no one actually recognizes what is happening. Yet despite this knowledge, we continue to seek scapegoats, and sometimes we find ourselves in the position of the one who is scapegoated. There is always someone who is annoying, who is always ruining everything, who is the cause of what's wrong with the world—or so it seems. Note that Girard does not say that the scapegoat is innocent in the sense that he or she has never done anything wrong; rather, the scapegoat is no more guilty of causing the disturbance in the group than anyone else. Everyone is part of the conflict—none is without sin—yet the scapegoat gets the blame.

When I was an undergraduate, I attended Binghamton University in New York, a "Public Ivy" where a commonplace left-liberal culture was dominant. There I encountered firsthand the intolerant ancestor of "wokeism" and cancel culture: political correctness, as it was called in those days. Some tried to shut down free speech and debate through intimidation and demonization. They sometimes succeeded because one has to pick one's battles.

A small number of us who were "other-thinking"—a group of Irish and Italian Catholics and Russian Jewish émigrés who didn't believe that America was irredeemably evil or that Marxism in any of its forms was the answer—resolutely banded together to publish a newspaper. In those days, it was still done by hand—cut and paste—with late nights in the copy room putting together proofs for the printer. We were called all sorts of names in public and in print: Nazis, fascists, racists—and worse, no doubt, behind our backs. We were, however, for the most part tolerated in the original sense of the term; that is, most ignored us, and those who cared put up with us and our crazy ideas. After all, we were pretty harmless: we had no power and held no positions of influence.

In one issue of *The Binghamton Review*, our editorial cartoonist decided to question the marketability of a degree from the newly emerging Gay and Lesbian Studies program. No one could have ever imagined that this cartoon was about to bring about the suspension of the group, a withdrawal of funding, and, after a long wait, a day in court. The editorial board—I was not among them—was hauled before the Student Government Association to determine whether they were guilty of thought crimes. While the offended accusers demanded "sensitivity training" for the perpetrators, who did not take their feelings seriously, the majority of the Student Government Association remained faithful to their authentic liberal credentials: the charges were dropped, and free speech won. I'm not sure if it would win today.

This story illustrates the qualities of a scapegoat: a tiny minority becomes the object of a community's opprobrium, which conditions the group to no longer see them as members of that community, but rather as deplorable outsiders. The process of demonization prepares for victimization. Fortunately, in this case, cooler heads prevailed: the Student Government Association remembered that education is meant to be a journey from immaturity to maturity, which entails unavoidable challenges to what one holds to be near and dear. It's part of growing up. Learning to deal with ideas that one finds uncomfortable is a necessary part of the search for the truth. Hard truths, as painful as they might be, are better than lies because the truth sets us free.

My close encounter with scapegoating gave me a new perspective on life. A decade later, I discovered that Girard had already described this and much more. His treatment of scapegoating not only explained these group dynamics but also proposed a theory of its origin. While many protohuman groups surrendered to mimetic rivalry and self-destruction, Girard surmises, some must have stumbled upon a solution that transformed the war of all against all into a war of all against one.

CHAPTER 8

The Scapegoat Mechanism

Girard refers to the sacrifice of one for the good of the many as the "scapegoat mechanism" or "single victim mechanism" (*mécanisme victimaire*). He refers to scapegoating as a mechanism because it follows a sequence that produces only two outcomes: success or failure. Girard maintains, however, that the mechanism is not deterministic for at least two important reasons: (1) variability of the scapegoat and (2) the possibility of failure. Regarding the first, the mob selects the victim arbitrarily, but not randomly.[1] Victims often exhibit irritating qualities (e.g., a troublemaker) or exceptional physical qualities (e.g., beautiful or ugly). Marginality at the top or bottom of society (e.g., the king or the poor) as well as nonmembership in the community (e.g., a stranger) also make one a more likely scapegoat, as does abnormal conduct. For example, King Oedipus was a foreigner (from Corinth), had a limp (having been maimed as an infant, which was meant to kill him), and was accused of socially unacceptable behavior (patricide and incest).

Secondly, if scapegoating is successful, then *no one* can be aware of it. The lack of unanimity means that the cathartic effects of scapegoating will not take place. The victim will be killed, but he will not function as a scapegoat because the vast majority of the community do not agree that that he was responsible for the

---

1. René Girard with Pierpaolo Antonello and João Cezar de Castro Rocha, *Evolution and Conversion: Dialogues on the Origins of Culture* (London: Continuum, 2008), 68–69.

crisis. This unanimity is spontaneous. Although it is possible that people can manipulate the group in the selection of a scapegoat, the group must not know that they have been influenced in this way. For the positive effects of the scapegoat mechanism to work, the group regards itself as innocent of blaming someone for their problems who is not the cause of their problems.

If the scapegoat mechanism *is* successful, then the community undergoes catharsis, a release from the mimetic fury, and a concurrent, seemingly miraculous reconciliation. However, the genuine source of this peace—namely, the elimination of the victim—must remain concealed from the group. The community cannot doubt its justice; it must honestly believe in the righteousness of its action. If significant doubts arise, there will be no release and no peace, but rather a new round of social contagion and violence, and the crisis will continue. This misapprehension[2] (*méconnaissance*) of the putative guilt of the victim and the putative innocence of the group is a necessary condition for the success of the scapegoating mechanism. The group must unknowingly misapprehend the truth that the scapegoat is no guiltier for the crisis than anyone else.

The following story illustrates the variability of the scapegoat and the possibility of failure. On a number of occasions in 1989 and 1990, culminating on January 25, a number of homes in Mbahe, South Africa, had been destroyed in lightning strikes, which local leaders and the community took as evidence of witchcraft. Arriving to the communal gathering late, Benedict Daswa—a Catholic principal of an elementary school who held an important status in the community as a husband and father of eight children, local leader, and lay catechist—contended that lightning is only a natural phenomenon. He consequently refused to pay a monetary contribution to hire a *sangoma*, a witch

---

2. Translated as "misapprehension" rather than "unconscious" in order to avoid any Freudian connotations. See Girard, 86–88.

hunter. (Compelling everyone to pay was a bit like having everyone cast a stone, inasmuch as everyone shared the guilt of the act of eliminating the witch.) Rather than seeing his conduct as an act of conscience and sincere Christian belief, Daswa's actions were interpreted as an act of hubris because he wouldn't go along with everyone else in their search for the witch behind the recent calamities.

Thus, a conspiracy to eliminate Daswa was set into motion. The search for the witch was deferred in favor of finding a moment to get rid of him. In effect, he became the scapegoat. The chance arrived on the same day that President F.W. de Klerk announced the unconditional release of Nelson Mandela and the unbanning of the African National Congress and other liberation movements. Apartheid was coming apart. In the midst of natural, political, and cultural upheaval—far beyond the immediate context of the lightning strikes—the community sought to expel its frustrations on a man who, in their view, was a troublemaker and irritant due to his Catholic faith and refusal to participate in the group's witch-hunting. His resistance was the straw that broke the camel's back.

On February 2, 1990, the Feast of the Presentation, or Candlemas, a group of young men ambushed the car of the principal. Escaping the stoning, he came to a nearby village, where the mob bludgeoned him to death as he prayed, "Father, receive my spirit."[3] At his funeral, the priests wore red, testifying to their belief that Daswa had died as a martyr to Christ. Later, the Archbishop of Cape Town, Stephen Breslin, succinctly summarized Daswa's legacy: "Aware of the fear caused by the practices of identifying witches, the harm this does to the fabric of social relations and the inevitable killing of innocent people, he was prepared to oppose

---

3. All information on Blessed Benedict Daswa is taken from "Martyr of Jesus Christ: Family Man, Educator, Community Leader, Catechist, Apostle of Life," https://benedictdaswa.org.za/.

this practice which still persists today, out of love for Christ and at the cost of his own life."[4] For this reason, he was beatified in 2015.

To stop scapegoating, Daswa became the scapegoat. In so doing, he conformed to Christ in a most exemplary manner. But even when the mob's fury polarizes on a scapegoat, the process is not necessarily successful. In the case of Daswa's murder, the community did not agree that it was the right thing to do. Divisions and fear lingered afterward.

But sometimes the process is successful. And for Girard, the success of the scapegoat mechanism—and the revelation of this mechanism through the Gospel—is the key to unlocking human history.

---

4. Bronwen Dachs, "Church beatifies South African teacher killed for resisting witchcraft," *The Catholic Register*, September 15, 2015, https://www.catholicregister.org/faith/item/20875-church-beatifies-south-african-teacher-killed-for-resisting-witchcraft.

CHAPTER 9

The Founding Murder

Mimetic desire, communal crisis, blaming scapegoats—when will it all stop? We don't know. But how did it all start? To this question—and Girard's understanding of human history—we now turn.

For Girard, scapegoating first took the form of human sacrifice as (1) the original lynching event, and then (2) its subsequent ritual repetition. The original event he calls the "founding murder," while its ritual repetition (which is treated in the next chapter) he calls "sacrifice."

In evolutionary terms, the scapegoat mechanism was an adaptation or corrective response to the mimetic desire's byproduct: unbounded violence. Girard argues that scapegoating was a contingent but necessary event in human evolution insofar as it did not have to occur at all (hence, contingent), but it did have to happen for human evolution to proceed (hence, necessary).[1] Girard hypothesizes that lapidation (death by stoning) was likely the earliest form of successful scapegoating because "there is no culture without the tomb and no tomb without a culture; in the end the tomb is the first and only cultural symbol. The above-ground tomb does not have to be invented. It is the pile of stones in which the victim of unanimous stoning is buried. It is

---

1. René Girard with Pierpaolo Antonello and João Cezar de Castro Rocha, *Evolution and Conversion: Dialogues on the Origins of Culture* (London: Continuum, 2008), 8.

the first pyramid."[2] Stoning, moreover, had the benefit of implicating everyone and no one in the murder, since all participated in the act but the final blow was unknown.

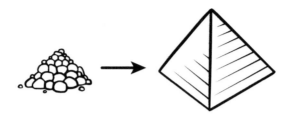

With this founding murder, the success of the scapegoat mechanism led to a transformation that was so sharp, and so swift, that the group believed its cause—both in terms of the conflict as well as its resolution—to be supernatural. Thus, its violence makes "the sacred" (*sacrificare* from the Latin *sacer facio*). In Girard's terms, "the sacred" refers not to God or the things of God, but to the result of the scapegoat mechanism—the deified victim, who is both the source of the conflict and the restorer of order through a new culture. The scapegoat mechanism transfigured the victim—first in a negative, violent fashion, then in a positive, benevolent fashion. The gods and goddesses are nothing other than superhuman beings dwelling in pantheons or families of gods with all the dysfunction of humanity.

These are the gods that the Greek philosophers ridiculed, speculating instead about a transcendent being such as Plato's mind or Aristotle's prime mover. The critiques of early sacrificial religion in India and China give further examples—the list is hardly exhaustive—of those skeptical of the reality and morality of the gods of the sacred. For Girard, however, biblical religion is unique in decoding the truth behind these gods. The Bible names this natural process of disorder and order "Satan": "Satan is mimetic contagion

---

2. René Girard, *Things Hidden since the Foundation of the World*, trans. Stephen Bann and Michael Metteer (Stanford, CA: Stanford University Press, 1987), 83.

as its most secret power, the creation of the false gods out of the midst of which Christianity emerged. To speak of the mimetic cycle in terms of Satan enables the Gospels to say or to suggest many things about the religions perceived by Christianity as false, deceptive, and illusory that they could not say in the language of scandal, the reconciling power of unanimous violence."[3]

When early Gentile Christians saw that they had escaped the worship of demons (false gods), they undertook a rational analysis of the complicity of the ancient gods with violence and the social order, whose values were strongly at odds with the Gospel—the most famous example of which is probably St. Augustine's *City of God*. Biblical revelation dethroned the gods and Satan, revealing them to be deceptive and illusory. This is not to say that they are without power or harmless; on the contrary, it is to underscore the danger that they cause (mimetic contagion) and from which they come (scapegoating).

Does this mean that Girard denies the existence of Satan as a spiritual being? This can at times seem to be the case: "To affirm that Satan has no actual being," Girard writes, "as Christian theology has done, means that Christianity does not oblige us to see him as someone who really exists. The interpretation that assimilates Satan to rivalistic contagion and its consequences enables us for the first time to acknowledge the importance of the prince of this world without also endowing him with personal *being*. Traditional theology has refused to do the latter."[4]

While this seems to be a flat-out denial of Satan as a personal being, Girard indicates that his claim should be understood strictly in the traditional Christian sense of the nonbeing of evil as a privation of the good: "The mimetic concept of Satan enables the New Testament to give evil its due without granting it any reality or ontological substance in its own right that would make

---

3. René Girard, *I See Satan Fall Like Lightning*, trans. James G. Williams (Maryknoll, NY: Orbis, 2001), 70.
4. Girard, 45. Emphasis in the original.

of Satan a kind of god of evil."[5] Put simply, Girard wants to avoid any hint of dualism whereby a god of good and a god of evil are in an eternal struggle as in, for example, Manichaeism or Zoroastrianism. Such a theology would necessarily be a lapsing back into the sacred in terms of mimetic rivalry and violence.

As a theological reality, however, Satan and other diabolical spiritual beings do exist. As creatures, they oppose God and those who belong to him. But the anthropological reading of Satan as mimetic rivalry and the scapegoat mechanism rehabilitates those New Testament texts that speak about Satan, which modern biblical scholarship has excluded from serious consideration, to a place of central significance.[6]

What is important to understand here is that in Girard's anthropological reading, "Satan" in the Scriptures points to the scapegoat mechanism from which the false gods spring: "Satan is the master of the single victim mechanism, and so he is the master of human culture, whose origin is none other than this act of murder."[7] To better understand these connections, we must look at the foundations of ancient religion and culture emerging out of the founding murder: ritual sacrifice, myth, and prohibition.

---

5. Girard, 44.
6. Girard, 32.
7. Girard, 87.

CHAPTER 10

The Foundations of Culture: Ritual Sacrifice, Myth, and Prohibition

The scapegoating event gives rise to a new community founding a new culture. The original event is reenacted through "ritual sacrifice" and remembered through "myth," and mimetic rivalry is hindered through "prohibition." Let's take a look at each of these three terms more closely.

RITUAL SACRIFICE

After the successful operation of the scapegoat mechanism, the community ritually reenacts the sacrifice to renew its sense of reconciliation. Girard believes that ritual is the first teacher of humanity because *repetitio est mater studiorum* (repetition is the mother of all study). Ritual repetition, therefore, is decisive for understanding cultural evolution. The perennial performance of ritual sacrifice educated the first human beings, thereby giving rise to all the major institutions that form human culture.[1] Contrary to anti-religious, social-scientific prejudices, which have their roots in the social contract and state of nature

---

1. René Girard, *I See Satan Fall Like Lightning*, trans. James G. Williams (Maryknoll, NY: Orbis, 2001), 89–91.

theorists of the Enlightenment (e.g., Thomas Hobbes, John Locke, Jean-Jacques Rousseau), it was religion—not philosophy, rational thinking, or spontaneous goodness—that formed the human race. Their imaginative retrojections of modernity into prehistory, and their unwillingness to acknowledge a striking difference between biblical and archaic religion, blinded the first generations of social scientists from seriously engaging the real source of humanization—namely, sacrificial repetition.[2]

Long before there were any secular institutions, whose origins depend on the desacralization or secularization that biblical religion causes, religion (or the sacred) was the mother of all culture. Ritual sacrifice created the social harmony and cooperation that stabilized desire-driven humanity. The sacrificial cult not only was a universal feature of ancient human cultures but also founded their worldviews.[3]

Girard also hypothesizes that ritual repetition may explain the origin of the first symbol, and therefore the emergence of language. The sacrificial victim is the original symbol for two reasons. First, the scapegoat introduces sameness and otherness. The scapegoating community sees itself as innocent (sameness) and the victim as guilty (otherness).[4] This contrast establishes difference, even if only inchoately. Second, in subsequent ritual reenactments, awareness grows that the freshly offered sacrifice not only is a new scapegoat/victim (otherness) but also signifies the original victim (sameness). This connects the sign or symbol to its meaning.[5] The new victim re-presents the original victim, while at the same time it is also a new victim/sacrifice.

    2. Girard, 88–89.
    3. Adolf Jensen, *Die getötete Gottheit: Weltbild einer frühen Kultur* (Stuttgart, DE: Kolhammer, 1966), 78.
    4. René Girard with Pierpaolo Antonello and João Cezar de Castro Rocha, *Evolution and Conversion: Dialogues on the Origins of Culture* (London: Continuum, 2008), 106–107.
    5. Earlier, Girard describes the victim as the signifier and the signified that constitutes all actual and potential meaning the community confers on the victim and through it on all things. See René Girard, *Things Hidden since the Foundation of the World*, trans. Stephen Bann and Michael Metteer (Stanford, CA: Stanford University Press, 1987), 103–104.

Borrowing a concept from the influential German philosopher Georg Wilhelm Friedrich Hegel, Girard describes the relationship between the scapegoating event and its ritual repetition as a "totality."[6] A totality is the end point of a historical process, which consists of a series of conflicts and resolutions (syntheses) between opposites (theses-antitheses). Each earlier conflict is subsumed by later conflicts and preserved in the final structure. The scapegoating event and its repetition constitute a closed network or system of references between the whole and its parts, as well as among its parts.[7] In other words, religion refers to a historical process in which language comes into existence by virtue of earlier developments.[8] Accordingly, ritual repetition, which rests on prehuman antecedents, precedes language because ritual repetition is a necessary condition for the emergence of the symbol, which makes possible language's building blocks—words that fuse together the sign and the signified, sound and meaning.

MYTH

With the appearance of language and the symbol, the community could record oral and written narratives of the mimetic crisis from their point of view. These reported to future generations the expulsion of the victim, his transmutation from demon to deity, and the subsequent foundation of a new cultural order. Myths "mute" the victims, silencing their voices underneath the shouts of the mob. They are essentially stories that misapprehend the founding murder and its ritual reenactments. They are not fairy tales but distorted accounts of historical events.

For example, Girard often returned to Oedipus in his writings because behind this figure from Sophocles' cycle of tragedies was a real human being who suffered expulsion. The banished

6. Girard, *Evolution and Conversion*, 106.
7. Girard, 148.
8. Girard, 37–38.

Oedipus is the scapegoat: the sin-bearer and the one who departs. We see in the myth how the scapegoat is both a poison (the cause of the disorder) and its remedy (restorer of order): it creates the crisis due to mimetic rivalry and then cures it through the *pharmakos* (Φαρμακος, a scapegoat ritually exiled and killed—from which we get the words "pharmacy" and "pharmaceuticals").[9] Girard calls this the "double transference," meaning that the scapegoating community first sees the victim as a demon who has inflicted a plague on them, and then, after the expulsion of the victim, comes to see the victim as a deity.

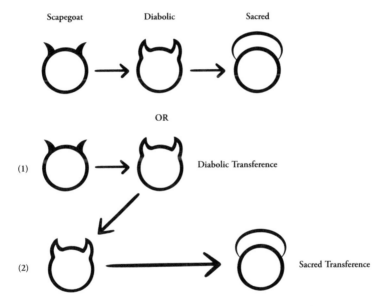

The original victim becomes a god who is both the plague-bearer (mimetic crisis) and culture-bringer (reconciliation through

---

9. René Girard, *Violence and the Sacred*, trans. Patrick Gregory (Baltimore, MD: Johns Hopkins University Press, 1979), 95. This word is significant insofar as its translation in Plato's texts conceals the hidden unity of the term—namely, that the *pharmakos* or *pharmakon* is simultaneously poison and cure. Plato applies this term, seemingly innocently, to the Sophists and Socrates, a point examined at length by Jacques Derrida in his article "La Pharmacie de Platon," in *La dissémination* (Paris: Seuil, 1972), 71–197, and approvingly cited in Girard, *Violence and the Sacred*, 295–297.

scapegoat mechanism). The Greek god Apollo, who was a real human being who underwent this "double transformation," exhibits both roles in *Oedipus Rex*.[10] After Oedipus murders his father and marries his mother, both unknowingly, thereby becoming the king of Thebes, Apollo the plague-bringer punishes the city for the king's transgressions. When Oedipus' sins become known, and the town turns against him and exiles him, Apollo the culture-bringer ends the plague because justice has been restored.

Through his literary analysis of medieval and early modern persecution texts, Girard tries to show that the only difference between them and earlier myths is the former's entirely unconvincing misapprehension of the scapegoating event.[11] They fail because they do not mythologize the scapegoats, but instead confidently, if naïvely, report the righteousness of the group against the guilt of the victim in stereotypical terms.[12] When properly deciphered, myths reveal the same story of a society in mimetic crisis, in which the surrogate victim is chosen on account of stereotypical signs of guilt,[13] rather than any genuine responsibility for the crisis, and expelled from the group to restore health and purity by ridding it of its pollution.[14]

Like a forensic anthropologist, Girard contends that myths refer to real events in which real human beings were murdered to restore peace. All human history, Haven summarizes, is "a crime thriller, in which the murderer escapes undetected, and the private investigator—in this case, Girard himself—is left only with hints and clues. Human society as a whole is guilty and complicit, hiding the body, and lying about what happened and how. The world's religions and

---

10. Girard, *I See Satan Fall Like Lightning*, 67.
11. René Girard, *The Scapegoat*, trans. Yvonne Freccero (Baltimore, MD: Johns Hopkins University Press, 1986), 1–11.
12. Girard, 12–23.
13. Girard, 17–21.
14. Girard, 24–25.

mythologies are the fibs it tells, both revealing and camouflaging what happened."[15]

PROHIBITION

Myths misapprehend and conceal the circumstances of scapegoating to maintain peace. Prohibitions arise for the same purpose—to promote peace—but carry out their function by forbidding those behaviors that incite mimesis. The new cultural order therefore sanctifies rules of conduct. In this lies the origins of law, the judiciary, and the apparatus of law enforcement. Inasmuch as mimetic desire naturally focuses on the neighbor and his possessions, prohibitions interrupt this desire by making the neighbor and his possessions distant and unapproachable, at least in a moral sense. Yet prohibitions alone, though directed to peace, are inadequate for achieving this end. As St. Paul's analysis of the Law demonstrates, prohibitions, too, can excite desire. Their proscriptive sense is unsatisfying. Only a positive model to imitate can fulfill the human desire for being.[16]

Once ritual, myth, and taboo became the regular features of the first human groups, thereby ensuring long-term survivability, other institutions such as agriculture,[17] domestication of animals,[18] medicine,[19] theater, philosophy, and kingship[20] developed. This vastly enriched cultural environment may have stimulated the brain's evolution due to the environmental pressures caused by

---

15. Cynthia L. Haven, *Evolution of Desire: A Life of René Girard* (East Lansing, MI: Michigan State University Press, 2018), 153.

16. Girard, *I See Satan Fall Like Lightning*, 13–14.

17. Girard, *Evolution and Conversion*, 121–122. He proposes that the ritual sites led to the first settlements, the domestication of animals, and the development of agriculture.

18. Girard, *Things Hidden since the Foundation of the World*, 68–73.

19. Girard, *Violence and the Sacred*, 287–289. He writes of the origins of medicine in terms of catharsis and the *pharmakos*. Cathartic medicines work by aggravating the symptoms, leading to a salutary crisis that brings about the recovery.

20. Girard, *Things Hidden since the Foundation of the World*, 51–68.

complexity of symbols and the burgeoning uses of languages.[21] In sum, therefore, religion opened the way for culture, which, in Girard's terms, is tantamount to the same thing. Only the process of evangelical demythologization makes a distinction between the sacred and the secular, between religion and culture, possible. Consequently, archaic religion is synonymous and coterminous with culture.

CAIN AND ABEL—AN ANTHROPOLOGICAL INTERPRETATION OF THE ORIGINAL SIN

Given these observations, Girard's theory also casts light on the story of Cain and Abel. For Girard, boundless human violence suggests an anthropological interpretation of original sin because humanity distinguishes itself from animals by its limitless vengeance, a conjunction of violence and intelligence.[22] (Girard maintains that most of his claims are anthropological, and therefore subject to the norms of scientific inquiry, but he also concedes that mimetic theory points necessarily to the reality of something beyond human beings, thereby having theological implications.)

He interprets the scriptural evidence from Genesis 4, the chapter after the story of the fall. The story begins with two brothers, the sons of Adam and Eve: Cain, the farmer, and Abel, the shepherd. The conflict arises over God's preference for Abel's animal sacrifice over Cain's plant offering. Cain envies Abel's relationship to God. God admonishes Cain to master his desire because sin personified lurks to ensnare him. Although Cain was free to choose to live in peace with his brother, he surrenders to mimetic rivalry and murders him. Fearing the vengeance of others—which implies that there are other human beings beyond the immediate family of Adam and Eve—God protects him with

---

21. Girard, *Evolution and Conversion*, 107.
22. René Girard, *Battling to the End: Conversations with Benoît Chantre*, trans. Mary Baker (East Lansing, MI: Michigan State University Press, 2010), 21.

the threat of divine vengeance, and finally, Cain founds the first human city/culture.[23]

Citing Jesus' denunciation of the Pharisees and scholars of the Law in Luke 11:50–51—"So that this generation may be charged with the blood of all the prophets shed since the foundation of the world, from the blood of Abel to the blood of Zechariah"—Girard contends that murders such as these should be taken to be historical events and not legendary. The connection between the foundation of the world and the murder of the prophets is the key. The founding murder brings forth a culture that places limits on violence (the threat of divine vengeance). Girard further argues that the murderer (or murderers, for he interprets Cain as representing a community and not only an individual, in a manner parallel to Jacob, "Israel," and the people Israel) learns a practical wisdom after his murder—namely, that violence must be brought under control through ritual sacrifice. Girard argues that this control over violence distinguishes Abel, who makes use of animal sacrifice to divert violence from other human beings, from his brother, Cain, who murders his brother because his plant offerings are insufficient to divert violence.[24]

Having murdered his brother and coming under the protection of divine vengeance, Cain founds the first city. Through numerous case studies, Girard shows that many founding myths come from historical events, acts of murder or expulsion. But in the case of the story of Cain and Abel, there is a twist: "The account of this murder is not a founding myth; it is rather a biblical interpretation of all founding myths. It recounts the bloody foundation of the beginnings of culture and the consequences of this foundation, which form the first mimetic cycle narrated in the Bible."[25] Girard argues that the Bible in general and the Gospels in particular transmit an accurate knowledge of violence: its origins

23. Girard, *I See Satan Fall Like Lightning*, 83–85.
24. Girard, *Violence and the Sacred*, 4.
25. Girard, *I See Satan Fall Like Lightning*, 83.

(mimetic desire), its operations (mimetic rivalry, conflict, murder), its corrective response (scapegoating), and its outcome (culture).

Girard's anthropological interpretation of the original sin corresponds to unbounded violence, the byproduct of the normal operation of mimetic desire. If one does not choose otherwise, mimetic desire descends into mimetic rivalry. Referring to Jesus' statement that "scandals must come" (see Matt. 18:7), Girard argues that even though individuals can avoid conflict, societies cannot. As imitation accelerates and dominates in more and more relationships, mimetic rivalries set off a snowballing effect that engulfs the group.[26]

In conclusion, Girard's account of humanization foresees repeating cycles of mimetic rivalry, crisis, sacrificial resolution/scapegoating, and the emergence of a new cultural order/religion over tens of thousands of years. In many cases, groups were consumed by their own violence. Only those groups that stumbled upon the scapegoat mechanism and developed religion and its cultural artifacts survived and indeed flourished. In this, natural selection eliminated many unfit human groups, leaving only those who practiced sacrifice to protect themselves from the ravages of unbounded violence. They did so through recourse to the *katéchon* (κατέχον), to which we now turn.

---

26. James Williams translates Girard's expression *emballement mimétique* as "snowballing." See Girard, 21–22.

CHAPTER 11

The Old Testament on the Kingdom and the Temple

In the prebiblical stage of humanity, the scapegoat mechanism not only destroyed its victims but also created culture. This creative potential, Girard argues, diminishes because of biblical revelation until it reaches its state of impotency today. The scapegoat mechanism can still destroy victims—indeed, in apocalyptic terms today—but it can no longer create. It has lost this power definitively, and it cannot be restored. To appreciate this development, this chapter traces the history of the interaction between the *katéchon* and divine revelation in light of two key institutions: the kingdom and the temple.

THE *KATÉCHON*[1]

Passing from prehistory into history, culture and civilization grew in complexity and scale even as scapegoating became sophisticated, surreptitious, and elusive. Archaic institutions put greater distance between their violent origins and their ongoing functions. For example, archaic religions substituted animals for human sacrifice, and even moved in the direction of spiritual sacrifices. Myths increasingly concealed the real victims under a veil

---

1. Girard refers to the *katéchon* under different rubrics in his writing. For example, he treats the same material under "Powers and Principalities" in *I See Satan Fall Like Lightning*, trans. James G. Williams (Maryknoll, NY: Orbis, 2001), 95–100.

of fantastic imagery, or simply forgot the true circumstances of the event, rendering them legendary. Hierarchy, social stratification, and class structure stabilized human relationships through sanctified, immobile social roles that curtailed mimesis through external mediation.

Girard categorizes the varied institutions that stabilize society as the *katéchon*, borrowing the term from 2 Thessalonians 2:6–7: "And you know what is restraining [*katéchon*] him now so that he may be revealed in his time. For the mystery of lawlessness is already at work; only he who now restrains [*katéchon*] it will do so until he is out of the way" (RSV-CE). Meaning both "the force which restrains" and "the one who restrains," *katéchon* refers to all human institutions and their agents that control violence through sanctioned violence. These institutions play a role against the mystery of lawlessness, which Girard equates with the mimetic crisis in which all differences collapse and everyone is consumed by conflict. The role of the *katéchon* is temporary, until "it is removed," which comes about by the spread of the Gospel.

Drawing upon the traditional interpretation of the *katéchon* as the Roman empire, Girard universalizes it to include not only religion, ritual, myth, and prohibitions, but also politics, war, law, economics, education, ethics, and morality. As human culture evolves, the *katéchon* transforms accordingly. Indeed, while the *katéchon*'s manifest functions may be self-evident (e.g., the *Pax Romana* ensured order and peace), its ultimate origins in scapegoating had to remain hidden—"misapprehended"—so that these institutions could possess the legitimacy required to function effectively. In order to appreciate the Bible's treatment of the *katéchon*, we will trace the history of the monarchy and temple.

THE OLD TESTAMENT

The story of Israel as a people begins with the family story of Abraham and Sarah. Later their grandson, Jacob/Israel, and his children migrated to Egypt during a famine. Departing from Egypt many years later, their descendants, the Israelites, and many others of mixed ancestry (Exod. 12:38) became a new nation, Israel, at Sinai. Although this covenant ordered Israel's relationship to God in terms of monolatry (worship of the one true God)—which later became explicit monotheism during the Babylonian exile[2]—the Israelites often succumbed to mimetic desire, which made them want what their neighbors had: a king and a temple.

A KING

Joshua brought the Exodus to its geographic conclusion with the arrival in the Promised Land. The conquest, however, did not happen as foretold. The Israelites mixed with the local population, breaking the boundaries set by the covenant. Until Saul, the only king in Israel was God. This set them apart from the other nations, whose rulers were generally god-kings such as their ancestors encountered in Pharaoh.

Yet, for explicitly mimetic reasons—they wanted to be like their neighbors (1 Sam. 8:4–5)—the Israelites demanded a human king. Despite God's severe admonitions about the rights of the king (1 Sam. 8:10–18), the people refused to listen: "No! but we are determined to have a king over us, so that we also may be like other nations, and that our king may govern us and go out before us and fight our battles" (1 Sam. 8:19–20). This demand contradicted God's stipulations in Deuteronomy 17:14–20, which stated that should the people wish to have a human king, his principal duty would be covenant fidelity, not warfare (Deut. 17:16–17).

When Zedekiah, the last king of Judah, went into the

---

2. "I am the Lord, and there is no other, besides me there is no god" (Isa. 45:5).

Babylonian exile more than five hundred years later, the author of the book of Kings judged that all of the kings were unfaithful (apart from David, Solomon, Hezekiah, and Josiah). The author of Chronicles includes a few more just kings. Overall, however, the human monarchy failed dismally. But there was hope that one day a Son of David would restore the kingdom.

THE TEMPLE

God did not ask for a temple but dwelt among his people in the ark of the covenant. King David, Saul's more successful successor, recovered the ark from the Philistines and brought it to Jerusalem, the newly conquered royal capital of the united kingdom of Judah and Israel. He must have thought that it would be fitting for there to be a royal temple to centralize the worship of God there also. Recounted in 2 Samuel 7—which is one of the key messianic texts—God reverses the offer, instead promising David a house over which his son will rule, declaring that this same son will build a house for the Lord. (In 1 Chronicles 22:8, David explains to his son, Solomon, that God did not permit him to build the temple because he had shed too much blood.)[3]

Since, early on, Solomon was renowned as the wisest man around (1 Kings 5:9–14), he fulfilled his father's dream of a royal temple (6–8) but failed to heed God's admonitions to be faithful to the covenant (9:1–9). The older and more foolish Solomon permitted his many foreign wives to introduce false worship in the royal temple (11:1–13). Since Solomon's son, Rehoboam, refused to grant tax relief to his subjects, ten of the tribes revolted to restore the kingdom of Israel. They built their own temple in their capital, Samaria, to which God later sent the prophet Amos to

---

3. And again, "But God said to me, 'You shall not build a house for my name, for you are a warrior and have shed blood'" (1 Chron. 28:3).

criticize its worship (Amos 5:21–27). A couple of centuries later, Jeremiah did the same in Jerusalem (Jer. 7:1–34).

The Assyrians destroyed Samaria, and later the Babylonians destroyed Jerusalem (2 Kings 25:9). But God took pity on Israel in exile. He anointed Cyrus (Isa. 45:1ff.), the Persian emperor, to defeat the Babylonians and end the exile. The emperor also allowed the construction of a second temple, which was only reluctantly built. Once again, it later fell to liturgical abuse under a Hellenistic ruler, Antiochus Epiphanes, who introduced pagan worship. Even the successful liberation of the temple under the Maccabees led to further divisions because their succeeding Hasmonean dynasty often meddled with the appointment of the high priests (though they were not of a priestly family). In the time of Jesus, the Sadducees ruled the temple in Jerusalem, but the Essenes at Qumran constituted an alternative temple community in opposition to the "wicked priest"—that is, the high priest—in Jerusalem. Herod the Great, the one who tried to murder the infant Jesus, magnificently expanded and richly adorned the temple. Jesus often conducted his ministry there, warning the Judeans of the peril of trusting in the majesty and might of the temple (Luke 21:5–6). Jesus knew that if the Judeans did not receive the Gospel as the way of peace, they would eventually go to war against Rome, which would destroy them (Luke 21:20–24).

PROPHETIC CRITIQUE

With the emergence of the kingdom and the temple, a new phase of prophecy commenced. Epitomized by Elijah, this new brand of prophets strongly criticized the covenant infidelity of the rulers, the people, and the cult. Repaid with persecution and death threats because they connected this faithlessness to injustice, the prophets prefigured Jesus' own suffering at the hands of the leaders and people. In fact, much of the Old Testament bears witness to this gradual revelation of the victim. Unlike myth, the Old Testament reports these persecution stories and sings psalms, both of which take the side of the victim. The story of Joseph is told from his point of view as a victim of false accusations (Gen. 37:2–50:5).[4] Job, the prebiblical patriarch, rejects the accusations of his comforters that his suffering is the result of his sin. Jesus decisively interprets the four canticles of the mysterious "servant of the LORD" in Isaiah (42:1–4, 49:1–6, 50:4–11, and especially 52:13–53:12) to explain his mission,[5] even as he does so in an unexpected way, by joining them to the Son of Man prophecy (Dan. 7:13–14). The novella about Susanna (Dan. 13:1–64) tells a story of the vindication of a young woman caught in the schemes of lascivious old men. Psalms 22, 35, 40, 56, 57, 69, and 70 speak of conflict or scapegoating events from the point of view of the potential victim.

The prophetic critique reached its climax in the ministry and teachings of Jesus. In him, the temple becomes his Mystical (Rom. 12:5) and Eucharistic (1 Cor. 10:16–17) Body, and the king is redefined to escape the lingering influence of the sacred and its mimetic origins, because his kingdom is not of this world (John 18:36). In other words, the origin of the kingdom is other than violence, the scapegoat mechanism, and the sacred; it is, instead, a matter of justice, peace, and joy in the Holy Spirit (Rom. 14:17) and is from the all-holy God.

The connection between the sacred and the holy, however, was not easily overcome. There is another side to the Old Testament that also reports God's threats of wrath, punishment, and violence, often in the same prophetic texts. These images and texts suggested to some people that there is truth to the opposition between the "Old Testament God of judgment" and the "New Testament God of mercy." From its start, this dialectical view has

---

4. Girard, *I See Satan Fall Like Lightning*, 106–120.
5. René Girard, *The Girard Reader*, ed. James G. Williams (New York: Crossroad, 1996), 154–158.

lurked in the shadow side of Christianity, requiring the Church repeatedly to reaffirm that the entire Bible—both the Old and the New Testaments—is the inspired Word of God. Therefore, no book may be eliminated for any reason, but must be accepted as part of God's communication to humanity. The problem of resolving these tensions lies with human beings, not with divine revelation.

The New Testament revelation so strikingly clarified the ambiguity of the Old Testament image of God and his relationship to violence that it may have contributed to the early heresy of Marcionism. Its author, Marcion, a second-century Roman priest, found it impossible to reconcile the two images of the Old Testament God of justice and the New Testament God of mercy. Instead of questioning his understanding of Scripture, he jettisoned the Old Testament altogether, as well as most of the New Testament outside of an edited version of Luke's Gospel and the Pauline corpus.[6] What was so shocking about this new revelation of God that led Marcion and those in his tradition—which returns again and again in the history of the Church—to seek a human solution to the paradoxes of revelation? It is the revelation of the nonviolent God and the innocence of the scapegoat.

---

6. Raymund Schwager, *Jesus in the Drama of Salvation: Toward a Biblical Doctrine of Redemption*, trans. James G. Williams and Paul Haddon (New York: Crossroad, 1999), 2–3.

CHAPTER 12

The Resurrection Reveals the Scapegoat Mechanism and the Innocence of the Victim

Girard strongly believes that the structural similarity between the Passion of Jesus and myths is necessary for the revelation of the scapegoat mechanism and the innocence of the victim. Both of these must occur if the world is to change. The Passion narratives describe a scapegoating event like any other. Yet what makes this one different is that it does not end with the death of the victim, but his Resurrection. Some might say, "But wait a minute: isn't the Resurrection an example of double transference, of the victim condemned who is subsequently held to be a god? That sounds like the Gospel." Yes—and that is Girard's point. It sounds like it, but there is a decisive twist: the Gospels proclaim Jesus to be innocent, not guilty. Recall the necessity of the moral unanimity of the crowd. As far as everyone could see—except for the tiny minority who saw it otherwise—the Crucifixion represented not only human but also divine justice: "For anyone hung on a tree is under God's curse" (Deut. 21:23). Yet on the third day, Jesus appears to his disciples—who would have also accepted the judgment against him as God's judgment—and declares that God has overturned the decision of the Sanhedrin, the crowd, and the Romans. In fact, he has revealed them to be guilty, and Jesus to be innocent.

Jesus offers his life on the cross in union with his Father to introduce a new power in the world that is stronger than mimesis and the scapegoat mechanism. That new power is the Spirit of Truth, the Holy Spirit, the Advocate, the Paraclete, who overcomes the misrecognition of the victim as guilty that makes the scapegoat mechanism hidden and effective. This is what we do when we scapegoat: we blame someone for our problems. But now we cannot believe it because it is unveiled for everyone to see. That's what has changed thanks to the Resurrection. It comes down to the truth: behind the lies of myth is the truth of the innocence of the victim.

Let's take a closer look, recalling that the Paschal Mystery encompasses the events we celebrate from Holy Thursday to Pentecost, and whose effects are without end. The Easter season is really one event in different moments: the vindication of the crucified at the Resurrection, the bestowing of the Holy Spirit in two moments (on Easter Sunday in John's Gospel and at Pentecost in Acts), the many appearances to strengthen the witnesses to the Resurrection, and the Ascension at which Christ hands on his mission to the one, holy, catholic, and apostolic Church.

EASTER

The soon-to-arrive sabbath rushed the proceedings at Golgotha. Having been ordered to break the legs of the thieves to hasten their demise, the soldiers discovered that Jesus was already dead. Joseph of Arimathea obtained the corpse and placed it in his own tomb. The proper execution of the burial customs had to wait.

On the third day, Mary Magdalene and two other women went to carry out their service only to find the tomb empty.

A little later, the Lord instructed her to bring the good news to his disciples, which she promptly did. That same day, the risen one walked with the disciples to Emmaus and then visited the disciples hidden behind locked doors, whereupon he offered peace, bestowed on them the Holy Spirit, and gave them the authority to bind and to loose. The Resurrection dissociated the true God from the gods of archaic religion (the violent sacred). There was no vengeance, but rather an invitation to repentance. As for Jesus, the Resurrection showed him to be the innocent one and the community and their leaders guilty, like every other scapegoating crowd. Truth changed the world, even if that truth meets resistance.

For instance, Paul quotes an early tradition of the Resurrection appearances in 1 Cor. 15:3–8 that does not mention Mary Magdalene at all. Whether this was due to the invalidity of women's testimony in Jewish law, the marginal status of women in general, or the desire to shield a prominent early disciple of Jesus from persecution and death is debatable. The latter scenario seems more likely when one recalls the martyrdom of Stephen in Acts 6–7, Saul's persecution and subsequent conversion in Acts 8–9, and the Roman client King Herod Agrippa's imprisonment of Peter in Acts 12 and his execution of James, the brother of John, in Jerusalem around 41–42 AD. The evangelists nevertheless righted this omission by the explicit inclusion of her witness. (Matt. 28:1–10, Mark 16:9–11, and John 20:11–18 report her encounter with the Risen Lord, whereas Luke 24:1–12 only reports her encounter with the two angels.) Their allegiance to the truth—for she is the Apostle of the Apostles—fostered a deeper understanding of human dignity because men and women are co-heirs to Christ's promises of eternal life. Changes were coming.

THE RESURRECTION REVEALS THE SCAPEGOAT MECHANISM AND THE INNOCENCE OF THE VICTIM

TRUTH-TELLING

This Christian urge to truth-telling has epochal effects in the practice of self-criticism (the examination of conscience and the sacrament of Penance) and in launching the scientific method.[1] To his frightened and confused disciples, Christ revealed the truth about the God who does not destroy his murderers or betrayers, but rather offers forgiveness, as well as the truth about humanity's relationship to violence. Through the Resurrection, the one whom the crowd and their leaders judged as a blasphemer (Matt. 26:65) and accursed by God (see Deut. 21:23), and whom the procurator, Pontius Pilate, representing the *katéchon* of his day, the Roman empire, condemned to death by Crucifixion (Matt. 27:26), was declared innocent.

Before the Sanhedrin (Acts 4:9–12), Peter, the first pope, rejoices in this miraculous revolution: "The stone that the builders rejected has become the chief cornerstone. This is the LORD's doing; it is marvelous in our eyes" (Ps. 118:22–23). After having told the parable of the wicked tenants, Jesus cited the same Psalm in reply to his audience's reaction (Matt. 21:42). The parable's context suggests that Jesus is teaching in the temple in Jerusalem just a few days before his Crucifixion. He foretells his own murder. Jesus will be the stone rejected, who is revealed to be the cornerstone, through the Lord's doing (the Resurrection). It is a wonder because it does not accord with the sacred logic of violence limiting violence (scapegoat mechanism), but rather introduces a holy logic that overcomes violence by self-sacrifice, forgiveness, and a new creation.

After the Resurrection, no one—not the murderers of Jesus or anyone else—is brought to a wretched end as predicted by those who answer Jesus' question (Matt. 21:40–41), thereby granting time for repentance. By the Resurrection, therefore, God forever overturned human misjudgment against Jesus on Good Friday. In

---

1. Grant Kaplan, *René Girard, Unlikely Apologist: Mimetic Theory and Fundamental Theology* (Notre Dame, IN: University of Notre Dame Press, 2016), 172.

so doing, God also declared all scapegoats innocent of the mob's accusations. As we have already seen, this is not to say that they are sinless as Jesus, but rather that they are no more guilty of the accusations of the mob than any other member of that same group who did not happen to be scapegoated.

AN UNEXPECTED CONFIRMATION

After September 11, 2001, the new atheists had their heyday. Christopher Hitchens' *God Is Not Great* cobbled together a catena of stories and arguments against religion. (Interestingly, in German, it was entitled *The Lord Is Not My Shepherd*, preferring an anti–Judeo-Christian title to the anti-Islamic one in English.) Five years earlier in his critique of liberal and leftist icons, Hitchens detected a deeper religious significance to hero-making: "It's the same vicarious impulse as makes people think—which is my main critique of religion—that they can cast their sins, say, onto a scapegoat figure, who will then take their sins away. Can you imagine a more repulsive idea? I cannot. Or a bigger abdication of what we call personal responsibility. It's a horrific idea, but it is preached by our churches."[2]

Hitchens rightly connects religion and scapegoating, but ironically, he critiques religion from the "view of the Gospels," as Girard calls it—that is, taking the side of the victim against the crowd and rejecting scapegoating altogether. Moreover, Hitchens, like the Gospels, confronts the group's responsibility for the lynching of the victim, depriving it of its mythic concealment. Therefore, both share the same concern for human responsibility. This convergence of views provides evidence for Girard's claim that there is one universal ethic in contemporary society: the

---

2. Christopher Hitchens, "A Dissenting Voice, with Christopher Hitchens," interview by Harry Kreisler, *Conversations with History*, University of California Television, September 19, 2002, video, 32:15–32:28, https://www.uctv.tv/shows/A-Dissenting-Voice-with-Christopher-Hitchens-Conversations-with-History-6725.

modern concern for the victim (more on this below). It is the one nonnegotiable in a sea of relativism.

That scapegoating might be "preached by our churches" also troubled Girard. Having difficulties with certain interpretations of sacrifice that understand Christ as a scapegoat, Girard initially defined sacrifice only in negative terms in *Things Hidden*.[3] He distinguished between historical or sacrificial Christianity, which remains firmly in the grips of the violent sacred, and essential or non-sacrificial Christianity, which represents Christ's authentic revelation. However, under the influence of his friend Raymund Schwager, he revised his view: "Today I have changed my mind.... Archaic sacrifice... turns against a third victim the violence of those who are fighting, and the Christian sacrifice... is the renunciation of all egotistic claiming, even to life if needed, in order not to kill."[4] Girard now contends that the proper distinction is not between sacrificial and non-sacrificial religion, but rather good and bad sacrifice.[5]

The effect of having revealed the truth at the heart of human culture and its violent origins gives rise to the circumstances in which we find ourselves today in the twenty-first century: "When our intellectuals, after the Second World War, and later with the collapse of the Soviet bloc in Eastern Europe, thought we were through with absolutes, they were simply wrong. Because the victimary principle of the defense of victims has become holy: *it is the absolute*."[6] Girard's remarks from nearly twenty years ago are even more true today as categorizations of victims and victimizers have grown exponentially. With financial, moral, and political capital to be gained, the complexities of human existence have

---

3. René Girard, *Things Hidden since the Foundation of the World*, trans. Stephen Bann and Michael Metteer (Stanford, CA: Stanford University Press, 1987), 224–262.

4. René Girard with Pierpaolo Antonello and João Cezar de Castro Rocha, *Evolution and Conversion: Dialogues on the Origins of Culture* (London: Continuum, 2008), 155.

5. René Girard, *Battling to the End: Conversations with Benoît Chantre*, trans. Mary Baker (East Lansing, MI: Michigan State University Press, 2010), 35.

6. Girard, *Evolution and Conversion*, 257–258.

been brutally simplified, opening the way for rash, cowardly, and cruel campaigns of intimidation and cancellation. The fury of social media and the internet has emboldened those who successfully claim victim status to become the new victimizers. For Girard, the Resurrection of Jesus sets off a revolution, the throes of which we witness to this day and will continue to witness until the end under the guidance of the Holy Spirit.

CHAPTER 13

The Holy Spirit, the Paraclete

Given the logic of the scapegoat mechanism—when it is successful, it is hidden, because the murderers misapprehend their innocence and the victim's guilt, and when it fails, the cathartic effect and reconciliation and peace are absent—Girard argues that its revelation demands a power stronger than the mimetic fury of the unanimous crowd: "To break the power of mimetic unanimity, we must postulate a power superior to violent contagion."[1] The dissenting voice declaring the innocence of Christ could not bear this testimony without intervention from outside of the system. For this reason, Girard must move beyond his naturalistic account and postulate the existence of a force outside of humanity that is able to do what no human being can do: end the misapprehension on which scapegoating depends.

This force is the third person of the Trinity. "The birth of Christianity is a victory of the Paraclete over his opposite, Satan, whose name originally means 'accuser before a tribunal,' that is, the one responsible for proving the guilt of the defendants."[2] At the Last Supper in John's Gospel, Jesus taught that the Holy Spirit is the defender of the accused and the Spirit of truth (John 14:16–17). In Girard's understanding, these complementary roles

---

1. René Girard, *I See Satan Fall Like Lightning*, trans. James G. Williams (Maryknoll, NY: Orbis, 2001), 189.
2. Girard, 190.

announce the truth of the innocence of the scapegoat and convict the world in regard to sin, righteousness, and condemnation (see John 16:8), thereby launching a humane revolution.

The Resurrection therefore changed everything, even if its effect has only slowly, but inexorably, destabilized the world of the sacred generated by the scapegoat mechanism. This new revelation of divinity is wholly independent of the sacred because it exists prior to it.[3] This God is not made through the scapegoat mechanism's transformation, through double transference, of the victim into a god; rather, he exists before there ever was anything, let alone a human race. The risen Christ distinguishes the all-holy God from the archaic gods of the sacred.

On Easter night, with the breathing of the Holy Spirit on the Apostles (John 20:21–22), Jesus commissions them to forgive sins (binding and loosing). Since "the Spirit takes charge of everything," Girard contends, "it would be false, for example, to say the disciples 'regained possession of themselves': it is the Spirit of God that possesses them and does not let them go."[4] The private Pentecost of Easter corresponds to the public Pentecost fifty days later when St. Luke describes the coming of the Spirit on Mary, the Apostles, and the disciples (Acts 2:1–4).

It all began three years earlier, when Jesus announced, "The time is fulfilled, and the kingdom of God has come near," and then commanded, "Repent, and believe in the good news" (Mark 1:15). The fulfillment of God's promise (with reference to both time and space) demands a response. One must choose to believe the "good news" (the Gospel). But what is the Gospel? Although in Christian usage it clearly refers to the message and meaning of Jesus Christ and the mission of the Church, it has an earlier history. In Greek, the *euanggelion* (*eu*, "good," and *anggelion*, "message"/"news") referred to messengers (angels) or heralds of the

---

3. René Girard, *Battling to the End: Conversations with Benoît Chantre*, trans. Mary Baker (East Lansing, MI: Michigan State University Press, 2010), 104.

4. Girard, *I See Satan Fall Like Lightning*, 189.

coming of a king. Hence, John the Baptist was Jesus' precursor, who foretold the advent of the Davidic Messiah, the redeemer of the failed institution of kingship. Christians evangelize by the proclamation that "Christ is risen." This is not simply a historical event, but rather a new state of existence: Christ is present and active in the world, thanks to the Holy Spirit.

The Holy Spirit, therefore, explains how the first Christians were able to bear witness to the crucified one as risen and innocent against the conviction of their society that he was guilty, a blasphemer, and cursed by God. The Holy Spirit, moreover, empowered the martyrs to testify with their lives. It also explains what Stephen meant in his speech when he said to his listeners, his fellow Judeans, "You are forever opposing the Holy Spirit, just as your ancestors used to do. Which of the prophets did your ancestors not persecute? They killed those who foretold the coming of the Righteous One, and now you have become his betrayers and murderers" (Acts 7:51–52). While this might sound like a rebuke against their moral or ethnic character, it might be better understood as an explanation for their inability to see the truth of scapegoating. Even with hints of this truth in the Old Testament, the power of the sacred was too great even for the chosen people to recognize what was going on—a condition, it should be noted, also present in the members of the Church.

Only through God's direct intervention in history did this change, as Jesus taught at Calvary—"Father, forgive them; for they do not know what they are doing" (Luke 23:34)—and as Peter proclaimed at Solomon's Portico in the temple precincts in his second speech: "Now, friends, I know that you acted in ignorance, as did also your rulers" (Acts 3:17). They acted in ignorance because of the concealing power of scapegoating. This is why Stephen, too, could pray for his persecutors: because they did not know what they were doing, remaining under the thrall of mimetic contagion. "Then he knelt down and cried out in a loud voice, 'Lord, do not hold this sin against them'" (Acts 7:60). Behind all of this stands the power of the Holy Spirit, who accompanies, guides, and inspires the Church in its mission to preach Christ crucified and risen despite opposition and resistance of those powers who are passing away.

As the chosen witness to Christ, the Church causes the greatest revolution in human history by exposing the fundamental anthropological truths of the violent origins of culture and by proposing salvation.[5] Girard predicts that this evangelical truth will inevitably delegitimize every institution that relies on scapegoating to preserve order and peace. Jesus' urgent desire "to cast fire upon the earth; and would that it were already kindled!" (Luke 12:49 RSV-CE) reveals the fire to be the Holy Spirit, the Paraclete. When the Church obeys the Spirit, then it fulfills Christ's own declaration that he came to bring division, not peace (Luke 12:51), for the peace of this world is the product of scapegoating. The Gospel paradoxically brings division and unleashes the possibility of violence because it undermines the moral credibility of the *katéchon* while simultaneously recommending Christ as the only model to imitate. He brings peace, but a peace free from scapegoating and violence: "Peace I leave with you; my peace I give to you. I do not give to you as the world gives" (John 14:27).

---

5. Giulio Meotti, "J'accuse of Rene Girard: The Audacious Ideals of a Great Thinker," in *Conversations with René Girard: Prophet of Envy*, ed. Cynthia L. Haven (London: Bloomsbury, 2020), 147–152.

CHAPTER 14

The Age of the Gentiles (Nations)

At the end of the introduction to *Battling to the End*, Girard writes, "History has meaning, and . . . its meaning is terrifying."[1] We are living through the result of the two-millennia process of the evangelical subversion of the sacred at the foundation of every human culture. Christianity effects apocalypse (revelation) in two senses. First, it reveals the truth about humanity's violent origins due to mimetic rivalry and the scapegoat mechanism, and consequently, it confronts humanity with a crucial choice in light of this disclosure: either imitate Christ or risk annihilation at our own hands. This unavoidable predicament comes from the great inversion that occurs: as humanity grows in knowledge of mimetism,[2] it loses control of its violence.[3] Yet, Girard argues, winning this battle is more important than a worldly victory (i.e., the cessation of hostilities): "We are thus more at war than ever, at a time when war itself no longer exists. We have to fight a violence that can no longer be controlled or mastered. Yet what if triumph were not the most

---

1. René Girard, *Battling to the End: Conversations with Benoît Chantre*, trans. Mary Baker (East Lansing, MI: Michigan State University Press, 2010), xvii.

2. Girard's term, *mimétisme*, is translated as "violent contagion" in *I See Satan Fall Like Lightning*, trans. James G. Williams (Maryknoll, NY: Orbis, 2001), 17 and as "mimetism" in *Battling to the End*. In either case, it refers to the process of mimetic rivalries accumulating in a society until they reach the breakpoint, the crisis in which the group expels the scapegoat or is consumed by its own violence.

3. Girard, *Battling to the End*, 143.

important thing? What if the battle were worth more than the victory?"⁴

What if the path is in fact the goal? Since scapegoating and the *katéchon* are less effective, what is needed is the heroic attitude to battle to the end, which "alone can link violence and reconciliation, or, more precisely, make tangible both the possibility of the end of the world *and* reconciliation among all members of humanity."⁵ The condition for the latter entails the possibility of the former. From this ambivalence we cannot escape, but in this situation, there is a real chance of reconciliation. This chapter describes the historical and spiritual process through which humanity has arrived at this pivotal moment.

History is accelerating to fulfill the Gospel's prophesies about wars and natural catastrophes that merge into apocalyptic visions because these—the events interpreted through the visions—signify the end of the sacred organization of the world (the *katéchon*). Today, natural catastrophes are increasingly the result of culture.⁶ Indeed, it is difficult to distinguish between nature and culture, as the rise of transgenderism and transhumanism suggest. Girard acknowledges that humanity has not self-destructed yet, but this is due in part to the waning but still real efficacy of the *katéchon*. It is a matter of time, however, before it will no longer hold back the violence that threatens to engulf the entire world. Humanity then will have to choose between conversion and self-destruction.

In Girard's view, the Gospels recount two cycles of history. The first tells of the life of Christ, culminating in the Paschal Mystery, which extends to the Second Coming; the second, which lies within the first, is the limited period of time between Christ's first coming and his return at the end of history. This second cycle Jesus called the "Age of the Gentiles" (see Luke 21:24), in which

---

4. Girard, xvii.
5. Girard, xvii. Emphasis in the original.
6. Girard, 114.

the anthropological and theological truths of the Gospel diffuse throughout the entire world, thereby effecting globalization.

In a real sense, the Age of the Gentiles recapitulates Israel's story: both Jews and Christians received the truth of God—one through the prophets, the other through Christ—but both failed to heed it.[7] Girard appears to believe that this double failure—the first of the Jews of a far smaller magnitude than that of the Christians (the murder of one man versus the mass murder of the Holocaust)—reveals something vital: the human race cannot be saved by knowledge alone because mimesis contaminates the truth and turns it to its own deadly ends. However, this conclusion can only be drawn when the Age of the Gentiles has run its course, thereby demonstrating over the centuries that humanity cannot create peace and reconciliation through the sacrificial means that once worked before Christ. In this respect, the final phase of the *katéchon*—spectacular in terms of its paradoxical progress and villainy—is modernity globalized.

Girard maintains that no society has ever exhibited so many advancements in the treatment of human beings as the West. Yet this same society is consumed with the desire to accuse and criticize itself for every lapse and abuse of human dignity, real or not. The West, in the name of multiculturalism and relativism, is even incapable of acknowledging its singularity and superiority over all cultures that remain mired in the sacrificial order: "Its superiority in every area is so overwhelming, so evident, that it is forbidden, paradoxically, to acknowledge the fact, especially in Europe."[8]

Girard foresaw cancel culture, in which persons learn to self-censor according to what is permissible to say based on current perceptions of who holds the balance of victim capital against those who are perceived as victimizers. The concern for the victim, which originally started off to vindicate the truth, now becomes

---

7. Girard, 112.
8. Girard, *I See Satan Fall Like Lightning*, 169.

an obstacle to truth-telling for fear of reprisal. Thus, the duplicity of myth creeps back into society. The following of Christ, which fearlessly acts out of truth, accepting the consequences in a way free from retaliation or vengeance, is the antidote. Let's see how we got here.

MODERNITY: THE *KATÉCHON* EVOLVES

Modernity refers to a new stage in the history of human mimesis under the influence of the Gospel. There is no hard and fast date that divides the so-called Middle Ages—a term applied to that period from scholars who lived much later in the nineteenth century—and "modernity," a term that comes from the Latin adjective *modernus*, meaning "of the present, up to date" and that was widely used in the late Middle Ages to describe a form of piety, the *devotio moderna* (an up-to-date or current style of prayer). A plausible schema places the transition from late medieval to early modern Europe in the fifteenth to eighteenth centuries; modernity in the late eighteenth to the mid-twentieth centuries; and the emergence of late or postmodernity in the mid-twentieth century. Therefore, when speaking about the evolution of the *katéchon*, we are describing a long process over centuries, which varies in time and place.

Broadly speaking, two related causes explain the trend to dissolve traditional constraints on mimesis in late medieval Europe: (1) their declining effectiveness due to the evangelical subversion of archaic religion (for example, the ineffectiveness of scapegoating due to doubt about the victim's guilt),[9] and (2) the intentional and conscious decisions to harness the productive and

---

9. Girard uses the example of Latin medieval persecution texts to show the intermediate step between myth and the Gospel. See René Girard, *Things Hidden since the Foundation of the World*, trans. Stephen Bann and Michael Metteer (Stanford, CA: Stanford University Press, 1987), 126–130; *The Scapegoat*, trans. Yvonne Freccero (Baltimore, MD: Johns Hopkins University Press, 1986), 1–11.

creative potential of mimetic desire.[10] Late medieval Italian capitalism gave rise to Western capitalism, which today has spread to the entire globe. At the same time, new forms of the *katéchon* appeared to manage the increasing risk of violence due to the harnessing of mimetic desire. These can be divided between two approaches. The first institutionalized safe forms of competition (e.g., market economy, consumerism, multiparty democracy, spectator sports, religious pluralism, the entertainment industry). The second conferred on the state a monopoly over violence in terms of the judiciary, law enforcement, and the military.[11] These forms, however effective they might be in the short to medium term, are not able to address the deep questions of human existence.[12] We see this with the widespread breakdown in the institutions of marriage and family as well as with doubts about the reality of male and female. Thus, although the modern and postmodern versions of the *katéchon* do control violence to an unprecedented extent, they cannot prevent and may even contribute to future mimetic crises.

In broad brush, this historical transition from late medieval to postmodern society includes a variety of revolutions that are interrelated and interdependent. First, due to the rise of trade and manufacturing, the middle class—"middle men" are mediators or traders—began to disrupt the tripartite social structure of nobility, clergy, and peasants (the social revolution). By the late medieval period, a concept of individualism, which is a precondition for modernity rather than its product, became sustainable (the anthropological revolution).[13] Moreover, medieval advances in state administration and the rule of law (thanks to the formation of law faculties at Bologna and beyond) prepared the way for later

---

10. Girard, *Battling to the End*, 61–62.
11. Michael Kirwan, *Girard and Theology* (New York: T&T Clark, 2009), 24–25.
12. Raymund Schwager, "Mimesis - Nachahmung," *Zeitschrift für Didaktik der Philosophie und Ethik* 19 (1997): 149–156, at 156.
13. For a thorough exposition of this thesis, see Larry Siedentop, *Inventing the Individual: The Origins of Western Liberalism* (Cambridge, MA: Belknap, 2017).

philosophical elaborations of new modes of political organization in terms of absolutist monarchies, social contracts, constitutions, and human rights, as well as international conventions on the rules of war and international trade (the political revolution). Emerging from the prophetic impulse of relentless criticism and truth-seeking, the scientific project gradually demythologized nature itself (the scientific revolution). The discovery of natural laws and processes made it possible to predict outcomes (the industrial revolution). The migration from agrarian communities to urban industrial societies necessitated geographic mobility that loosened familial and local ties (the urban revolution). With the recent expansion of computational powers, predictive control of laws and processes have greatly increased dominance over nature, including human beings (the information revolution). Lastly, the prodigious multiplication of desirable goods has pacified mimetic desire through abundance (the consumer revolution). Girard argues, however, that the proliferation of objects reduces their desirability, paradoxically contributing to a pervasive "throwaway culture," as Pope Francis often calls it[14]—in which "one buys objects with one hand, and throws them away with the other—in a world where half of the human population goes hungry."[15]

THE MODERN CONCERN FOR THE VICTIM

The brief foregoing summary raises the question: Why did this occur? Hidden under the fascination with technology, science, and ideology is the true cause of these revolutions—namely, the

---

14. "Human beings are themselves considered consumer goods to be used and then discarded. We have created a 'throw away' culture which is now spreading. It is no longer simply about exploitation and oppression, but something new. Exclusion ultimately has to do with what it means to be a part of the society in which we live; those excluded are no longer society's underside or its fringes or its disenfranchised—they are no longer even a part of it. The excluded are not the 'exploited' but the outcast, the 'leftovers'" (Francis, *Evangelii Gaudium* 53, apostolic exhortation, November 24, 2013, vatican.va).

15. René Girard with Pierpaolo Antonello and João Cezar de Castro Rocha, *Evolution and Conversion: Dialogues on the Origins of Culture* (London: Continuum, 2008), 58.

modern concern for the victim. The Argentine Salesian priest and artist Padre Eduardo Meana sings in "En mi Getsemaní" (In my Gethsemane),

> It is neither in words nor in promises
> where history has its secret engine.
> It is only love, on the cross matured,
> the love that moves the whole universe.[16]

Meana puts it poetically when he claims that the love matured on the cross is the "secret engine" of history. Similarly, Girard believes that this Christian conviction is the provenance of the most humane features of modernity.

While the Resurrection casts in doubt all the sacred structures that depend on scapegoating to sustain peace and prosperity, "the idea of a society alien to violence goes back clearly to the preaching of Jesus, to his announcement of the Kingdom of God."[17] In the vision of the universal judgment (Matt. 25:31–46), the Son of Man passes sentence according to the practice (or non-practice) of the works of mercy: "Truly I tell you, just as you did it to one of the least of these who are members of my family, you did it to me" (Matt. 25:40). While there is open debate among biblical scholars about the original identity of the "least of these," the subsequent Christian interpretation leaves no doubt that no one—Christian or not—is excluded from this identification with Jesus; whatever one does or fails to do, one does to him.

A series of moments and acts underscores Jesus' ever-intensifying identification with humanity. First, the eternal Word becomes flesh and dwells among us. Then, at his baptism in the Jordan, he identifies with sinners, though he is not a sinner himself. In Matthew 25, Jesus identifies with persons who suffer want

---

16. "No es en las palabras ni es en las promesas / Donde la historia tiene su motor secreto / Solo es el amor, en la cruz madurado / El amor que mueve a todo el universo" (Eduardo Meana, *Más allá de mis miedos* [Beyond My Fears], Inspiración, 1999; translation mine).

17. Girard, *I See Satan Fall Like Lightning*, 164.

and need. Finally, through his death on the cross, he identifies himself with all the victims of the scapegoat mechanism. This compelling message radically reordered the Christian understanding of the commandment to love your neighbor as yourself (Lev. 19:18) through the New Commandment to love one another as Jesus loves us (John 13:34–35). That means to love your enemies (Matt. 5:44; Luke 6:35) and forgive their sins.

THE CHRISTIAN PRACTICE OF CHARITY

Love for the poor, a deeply embedded value in the Old Testament totally at odds with Greco-Roman mores, puts into practice Jesus' New Commandment. Why? During the exile, when there was no access to the temple, almsgiving gained a new status as a valid substitute for a sacrificial offering that was pleasing to God and atoned for sin (e.g., Tob. 14:10; Sir. 3:14, 30; 29:12). This substitution for sacrifice arose among the deportees of the Assyrian conquest of Israel (722–721 BC) and the Babylonian conquest of Judah (c. 580 BC), whose generosity became a confession of faith in God's goodness: "Whoever is kind to the poor lends to the LORD, and will be repaid in full" (Prov. 19:17).

The Fathers of the Church universally agreed about the intrinsic connection between the Eucharistic sacrifice and almsgiving: "Placing an offering on the altar is like putting money in the hands of a poor person. Just as God did not need the sacrifice of animals in the temple but desired that we give them to Him for our own benefit, so God does not need the alms we give but demands them from us in order that we might have some concrete means of displaying reverence."[18] Christian charity not only relieved the poor of their want but also manifested concretely the faith of the giver as something more than empty words.

---

18. Gary A. Anderson, *Charity: The Place of the Poor in the Biblical Tradition* (New Haven, CT: Yale University Press, 2013), 151.

THE AGE OF THE GENTILES (NATIONS)

From the beginning, Christian charity delegitimized discrimination and prejudice through its care for the destitute, widows, slaves, orphans, the sick, the old, strangers, and travelers. It educated men and women, boys and girls alike, as all share a common sacramental path to salvation in Christ: "As many of you as were baptized into Christ have clothed yourselves with Christ. There is no longer Jew or Greek, there is no longer slave or free, there is no longer male and female; for all of you are one in Christ Jesus" (Gal. 3:27–28). The practice of charity in the ancient world set Christians apart from their pagan neighbors, whose values esteemed power, strength, and success, showing little regard for those who were excluded or vulnerable. As Christians became more numerous and influential, new kinds of charitable institutions came into existence to dispense mercy, and legislation was enacted to restrict activities that diminished or denied human dignity.

Even when Christians failed to live up to their convictions due to compromises with a given political (sacrificial or sacred) order, prophetic reformers, such as St. Francis of Assisi, St. Catherine of Siena, St. Óscar Romero, and St. Teresa of Kolkata, appeared. Ironically, even anticlerical or anti-Christian movements sometimes advanced this core conviction. Today, one may at the same time affirm that the world is both the best and worst of all worlds, because while there are more victims than ever before (legalized abortion leads the way), the opposite is true as well: never have so many victims been spared violence.

Girard recognizes mimesis' predictable conquest of the modern concern for the victim through its weaponization: "This ideal does not diminish to the extent that Christianity recedes; to the contrary, its intensity increases. The concern for victims has become a paradoxical competition of mimetic rivalries, of opponents continually trying to outbid one another."[19] Paul does

---

19. Girard, *I See Satan Fall Like Lightning*, 164.

something similar when he speaks about how the Law, which is holy and good, is not able to help the sinner overcome sin, but rather aggravates temptation (Rom. 7:7–25). In both cases, what is good can be overwhelmed by what is not, leaving human beings in an ambivalent place.

GLOBALIZATION

Girard contends that the modern concern for the victim—the "secular mask of Christian love"[20]—founded the first planetary culture. "Globalization," which emerged out of the collapse of European imperialism, the Cold War confrontation between East and West, and the post-1989 American global hegemony, refers to a historical stage in which this core value of the Gospel assumed normative value for the entire world. In Girard's opinion, it was the genuine force driving this movement.[21] At the same time, globalization also refers to the emergence of the possibility, hitherto unknown, of the annihilation of the entire human race. Globalization therefore shifted the theater for mimetic desire from the neighborhood in premodern society and the nation-state in modernity to the whole Earth.

Bound together by the internet, mass media, global popular culture, economic interdependence, and international trade, and mixed up by the mass movements of peoples, traditional external mediation is rapidly diminishing in scope and effectiveness (Celebristan is declining). Globalization as the spread of modernity to all peoples leaves everyone vulnerable to internal mediation (Freshmanistan is ascending). Excited by the proximity and abundance of tantalizing choices, desire turns to resentment when, in frustration, it cannot obtain the object of desire, or to boredom when excessive availability of objects reduces their desirability.[22] Agitated

20. Girard, 165.
21. Girard, 165–166.
22. Girard, *Battling to the End*, 80–81.

THE AGE OF THE GENTILES (NATIONS)

by these obstacles, mimetic rivalries spread contagiously, like the new phenomena of plagues transported by airplanes around the globe, threatening to consume not only societies but now the entire world. Globalization's concern for the victim has increased the chance for global self-destruction.

CHAPTER 15

"Gaudium et Spes, Luctus et Angor..."

The Second Vatican Council's Pastoral Constitution on the Church in the Modern World is commonly known by its Latin name, *Gaudium et Spes* ("Joy and Hope"). Yet to stop there, without reading the whole sentence, inadvertently gives the false impression of an anachronistic optimism of Tomorrowland at Disneyland (the one in California). Balancing joy and hope with *luctus et angor* ("griefs and anxieties"), the constitution presents a realistic analysis of the great distance that humanity must still traverse if it is to realize its dignity and purpose in the lives of everyone. Nevertheless, humanity is not abandoned: "Inspired by no earthly ambition, the Church seeks but a solitary goal: to carry forward the work of Christ under the lead of the befriending Spirit. And Christ entered this world to give witness to the truth, to rescue and not to sit in judgment, to serve and not to be served."[1] Girard's vision can also seem harrowing, but it has a solitary goal: to give witness to the truth.

As I was rummaging through boxes of my old vinyl records in my parents' garage recently, I found the twelve-inch single "World Destruction" by the punk-funk fusion project Time

---

1. *Gaudium et Spes* 3, in *The Word on Fire Vatican II Collection*, ed. Matthew Levering (Park Ridge, IL: Word on Fire Institute, 2021), 217.

Zone. With a strong percussion beat and refrain—"This is a world destruction, your life ain't nothing / The human race is becoming a disgrace"—the Sex Pistols' lead singer, Johnny Lydon, and the rapper, Afrika Bambaataa, capture mimetic contagion. In this memorable mishmash of politics, religion, and the looming threat of doom, accompanied by synthesizer and guitars, screaming, and shouting, one is left with the impression that there is a total collapse of differences; it is now entirely unsure if there are any good guys. A mimetic crisis is world destruction when everything falls apart. But there is still a chance: "If we don't start to look for a better life / The world will be destroyed in a time zone!"[2] We do, however, have a choice, because mimetic rivalry is not inevitable for individuals. Unlike societies, mimetic rivalry does not have to engulf us. But ominously, Girard does seem to believe that although a global crisis may be postponed, its delay only intensifies the final violent outcome.[3]

With the fall of the Berlin Wall in 1989, there was much optimism—a lot of *gaudium et spes* without the *luctus et angor*—regarding the future. Francis Fukuyama's "The End of History?" in the neoconservative journal *National Interest* provoked much debate about whether humanity had reached a watershed.[4] Fukuyama suggested that humanity had arrived at the end of history because ideologies were exhausted, leaving liberal democracy as the final stage of human development. Fukuyama borrowed the phrase "the end of history" from Hegel's lectures on world history. Using the German word *Ende*, it might be clearer to render "end" as "goal" or "aim" of history. Hegel argued that the French Revolution universalized the values of equality, liberty, and fraternity and that these are the aim

2. Time Zone, John Lydon, and Afrika Bambaataa, "World Destruction," Cinevu/Nu-Media, 1984.

3. René Girard, *Battling to the End: Conversations with Benoît Chantre*, trans. Mary Baker (East Lansing, MI: Michigan State University Press, 2010), 34–35, 43, 45–46, 101.

4. Francis Fukuyama, "The End of History?" in *The National Interest*, no. 16 (Spring 1989): 3–18.

of world history. Marx adapted Hegel's idealist philosophy of history to his materialist views and believed that communism was the true aim of human progress.

Girard detects in all modern myths of progress (liberal or not) an unwillingness to face their violence. Ideologies are not violent per se; people are. Ideologies are the updated version of myths, which "provide the grand narrative which covers up our victimary tendency. They are the mythical happy endings to our histories of persecutions. If you look carefully, you will see that the conclusion of myths is always positive and optimistic."[5] In contrast to ideologies, "the Gospel does not provide a happy ending to our history. It simply shows us two options (which is exactly what ideologies never provide, freedom of choice): either we imitate Christ, giving up all our mimetic violence, or we run the risk of self-destruction."[6]

The unhappy ending of the Gospel subverts the myth of progress, thereby freeing us from its inevitability and giving us a genuine choice. Through the revelation of what is really going on behind the sacred, Christian demythologization has rendered the scapegoat mechanism and the instruments of the *katéchon* sterile because violence no longer has the capacity to create anything: "It is finished. It is impotent. Thus, this is real anarchy."[7] Girard means that the culture-producing potency of scapegoating is past. The instruments of the *katéchon* wear down under the implacable erosion of mimetism. Among those fading instruments, Girard

---

5. René Girard with Pierpaolo Antonello and João Cezar de Castro Rocha, *Evolution and Conversion: Dialogues on the Origins of Culture* (London: Continuum, 2008), 169.

6. Girard, 169.

7. Girard, *Battling to the End*, 116.

includes war,[8] law,[9] rationalism,[10] ethics,[11] and archaic religion (the sacred).

Consequently, in light of the Gospel prophecies (Matt. 24; Mark 13:19–20), humanity must pass through the current ordeal ("griefs and anxieties"), deprived of the guide markers of the sacred, because once-reliable explanations for human existence are exhausted, hearts have grown cold, and the violent contagion spreads globally. Adverting to the suffering of the elect in Mark 13:19–20, Girard recalls Christians to their true end as disciples: "The interminable descent, the corruption that constantly reduces the number of Christians, is dangerous for the elect. However, the small number must hang on to the end, despite the false prophets."[12] Believers must "battle to the end," refusing to give up hope despite all the signs to the contrary.

HOPE

One of the most innovative sci-fi series, *Babylon 5*, gives us a poignant image of hope. The episode "The Long Twilight Struggle" recounts the tragic end of the Narn-Centauri war. The charismatic Narn ambassador, G'Kar, receives sobering news from G'Sten, his uncle, that the war is going very badly for the Narn. Without taking grave risks, all will be lost. The noble G'Kar replies, "Then all

---

8. Girard, xii.

9. "Law itself is finished. It is failing everywhere. . . . Violence produced the law, which is still, like sacrifice, a lesser form of violence. This may be the only thing human society is capable of. Yet one day this dike will also break" (Girard, 108).

10. "Rationalism, the latest form of rituals, has failed to manage violence because it denies it, veils its eyes to the truth" (Girard, 68). Girard's assertion makes sense in light of his critique of the modern concept of the individual as a point of departure for thinking, from which rationalism develops. "Mimetic theory contradicts the thesis of human autonomy. It tends to relativize the very possibility of introspection: going into oneself always means finding the other, the mediator, the person who orients my desires without my being aware of it" (Girard, 10). If mimetic theory is correct, then the thinking subject cannot start with itself because the other has already influenced one to perceive the other's desires as one's own. However, there is no such absolute beginning in human beings.

11. Girard, 23.

12. Girard, 115.

is lost," to which G'Sten replies, "There is always hope." (Interestingly, the risky action does fail, and their home world does indeed fall to ruthless occupation, but hope endures in a new Christlike role for the character of G'Kar.) Girard also believes that despite the crucial moment at which humanity has unavoidably arrived, there is still hope, if we start to look "for a better life."

Girard sees hope precisely in the willingness to recognize the truth about violence. Apocalyptic thinking restores meaning and sustains hope, where others find only despair and nihilism. The apocalypse definitively demythologizes the wrath of God as nothing other than the violence of man against man, which in the end persecutes Christ himself. "Why do you persecute me?" the risen Lord interrogates Saul, the pious Pharisee on a mission from the high priest to arrest Jesus' followers (Acts 9:4). The repentant Saul joined the repentant first pope in professing the newness of our situation: "The Resurrection empowers Peter and Paul, as well as all believers after them, to understand that all imprisonment in sacred violence is violence done to Christ. Humankind is never the victim of God; God is always the victim of humankind."[13]

Instead of vengeance and violence, God offers a forgiveness that grants a peace not of this world (John 14:27)—that is, a peace not purchased at the price of others' lives. In so doing, the Gospel announces the imminent adulthood of the human race in terms of its responsibility to choose "a better life." In this, Christ completes humanization because he reveals the innocent victim and challenges the human race to take responsibility for its actions, admitting the violent foundations of culture and resolving to imitate him in his positive mimetic relationship to his Father.

Girard therefore proposes an alternative to German philosopher Immanuel Kant's view of human development, which supposed that the Enlightenment would cause human maturity.

---

13. René Girard, *I See Satan Fall Like Lightning*, trans. James G. Williams (Maryknoll, NY: Orbis, 2001), 191.

In his 1784 essay "Answering the Question: What is Enlightenment?" Kant describes human existence as the passage from "self-imposed infancy" to the willingness to face the world fearlessly as adults ought to do. The term emphasizes the individual's responsibility for this state of dependency. Further, "infancy" (*Unmündigkeit*) refers to a specific legal status known in his day—namely, that of a minor under the authority of his parents. *Unmündig* recalls the Latin *infans*, "unable to speak." Thus, one who cannot speak for oneself is under the domination of another—hence the need to promote self-expression and free speech to exhibit one's autonomy and to emancipate oneself from authority.

The Kantian ethos depicts adults and children as emblematic of two existential states. Once, humanity lived as frightened, naïve children protected from the truth by the illusion of religion and the firm hand of the king. Now, it was time to cast off these infantile notions—to "dare to know" (*sapere aude!*)—and to see the world not through the Bible or tradition but through telescopes and microscopes. This ethos contributes to the modern preference for Gnosticism, the ancient heresy promising salvation through knowledge (science) and technology. ("Trust the experts" and "follow the science" might be responsorial psalms of this religion). Modernity promised worldly salvation, a historic transformation, an earthly paradise. It cast the Church and religion in the role of the oppressive parent, whom one must overcome and dethrone if one wishes to be free.

Putting aside the optimistic claims of Kant, Girard maintains that the Gospel asserts that this opportunity for reconciliation has only appeared once in history and that, as the apocalyptic texts imply, it was not seized. Thus, though reconciliation is in principle possible, it has proven impossible.[14] Therefore, the Second Coming of Christ—the closing of the Age of the Gentiles—will publicize the verdict that "the adulthood of humanity, which he

---

14. Girard, *Battling to the End*, 48.

announced through the cross, failed."[15] The human race cannot be saved by its own efforts, even when guided by the truth. Knowledge alone is insufficient. Apocalyptic thinking, on the other hand, has the courage to acknowledge what modern wisdom does not: reason, identity, and fraternity will inevitably fail to achieve an immanent salvation of humanity because mimesis is always stronger.

Indeed, this argument finds a parallel in the life of Christ, who for three years preached the Gospel and performed healings, miracles, and exorcisms, but to no ultimate effect. The mimetic crisis that came to a head on Good Friday included Judas' betrayal, the Apostles' abandonment, and Peter's threefold denial. Only a few people—who, in the eyes of the world, were also meaningless—did not succumb: Mary, Mary the wife of Clopas, Mary Magdalene, and John, who stood at the foot of the cross. Mimetic reciprocity that escalates to the extremes cannot be eliminated. It remains inherent in the character of human desire.[16] Yet for individuals, as opposed to groups, there is hope because one is free to choose not to descend into negative mimesis, to become a rival, to reciprocate and retaliate, but rather to choose positive mimesis through a model, who is at "the right distance."[17]

---

15. Girard, 105, 118–119.
16. Girard, 101.
17. Girard, 123.

CHAPTER 16

The Right Distance

Though Girard firmly maintains that mimesis is the implacable law of human behavior that inevitably spreads a contagion around a society, the same cannot be said for each person because one is free to choose. "In communities, there are so many people that it would be statistically impossible for mimetic violence not to be present, but the individual isn't bound hand-and-foot to mimetic desire. Jesus himself was not. To talk about freedom means to talk about man's ability to resist the mimetic mechanism."[1] Mimesis does not determine the outcome of individual choices; human beings do. Equipped with knowledge and the right model, human beings can and do resist the reciprocity that leads to violence. After the cross and its demythologization of the cultural order, people do enjoy a genuine free choice to succumb to or resist negative mimesis.

The concept of fate found in many archaic religions is absent in biblical religion,[2] which implies freedom and responsibility as a corollary to the goodness of God. Conversion consists of this freedom of choice and the knowledge of the operation of mimesis made available through Christ. Therefore, coming to recognize one's complicity in persecution and violence against others, one no longer claims innocence, but rather confesses one's guilt, the precondition of the forgiveness of the crucified and risen one. The

1. René Girard with Pierpaolo Antonello and João Cezar de Castro Rocha, *Evolution and Conversion: Dialogues on the Origins of Culture* (London: Continuum, 2008), 160.
2. Girard, 142.

admission of guilt elicits the resolution to adopt a new way of relating to others that does not escape mimesis but changes one's interaction with it: "To convert is to take distance from the corrupted sacred, but it does not mean escaping from mimetism."[3] Conversion therefore means to use knowledge of mimesis to opt for the right kind of mimesis.

Luke Burgis compares sympathy and empathy, both coming from the root, *pathos*, which in Greek means "feelings." Sympathy, "feeling together," Burgis observes, is especially susceptible to mimesis: "Have you ever been part of a group that begins a conversation about something and rapidly coalesces around some form of agreement . . . ? You find yourself nodding along, smiling, maybe even agreeing out loud. But a few minutes later, or when you get home later that night, you think, *Hold on . . . do I really agree with that?*"[4] In these ordinary scenarios, we find ourselves ineluctably moving in a direction we would not deliberately choose. Only if we get hold of ourselves can we thwart the powerful attraction to agree with the group. (If you doubt this force, try staying seated at the end of a concert and not applauding.) We can choose to be silent, but then, doesn't silence mean consent? Or does it? While we might risk giving the impression we agree, we may also avoid a needless conflict. Of course, there are situations when conflict cannot, and should not, be avoided.

Burgis advises empathy as a surer approach to diffuse mimetic contagion because it "is the ability to share in another person's experience—but *without imitating them* (their speech, their beliefs, their actions, their feelings) and *without identifying with them* to the point that one's own individuality and self-possession are lost."[5] Empathy enables one, for example, to listen to hurt and

---

3. René Girard, *Battling to the End: Conversations with Benoît Chantre*, trans. Mary Baker (East Lansing, MI: Michigan State University Press, 2010), 106.

4. Luke Burgis, *Wanting: The Power of Mimetic Desire in Everyday Life* (New York: St. Martin's, 2021), 156. Emphasis in the original.

5. Burgis, 156. Emphasis in the original.

angry people without being drawn into their feelings, even when one is the overt target. One receives negative judgments but does not identify with them. One is not drawn into the maelstrom of mimetic contagion when the urge to defend oneself arises spontaneously. Rather, by listening calmly and carefully, the other person starts to feel acknowledged and accepted. Genuine reconciliation eventually can follow because now both can communicate honestly, without fear of rejection or harm, recognizing that feelings and perceptions are not oracles of truth, but must be purified by truth.

The same truth applies to our desires. Burgis distinguishes between "thin desires"—those that leave us feeling empty even when we accomplish them—and "thick desires" that fill us with abiding, enduring happiness. Thin desires are mimetically driven and mostly unreflective. They are more often associated with younger people who are simply less practiced, both in experience and in wisdom. As one grows older, gaining more experience with the exercise of desire, one learns through reflection and evaluation that many desires are ephemeral or passing—pleasurable for the moment, but utterly forgettable. Every child knows this from Christmas morning: the longed-for toy or game by evening often seems to lose its luster as other objects seem more attractive.

Thick desires, therefore, must be cultivated, and there is no mythic "inevitable progress" whereby we will stably possess thick desires. The polarity between thin and thick desires pulsates throughout our lives, and we never leave this tension behind. But we can deliberately choose to discover our thick desires. Since specific thick desires are not obvious for most people, Burgis recommends recalling an event or success in your life that can disclose what deeply motivates you and what brings happiness. He calls these "Fulfillment Stories," which have three essential elements: it is an action in which you exercised your agency (your ability to choose and to do something); you believe you did it well; and it brought you a sense of fulfillment.[6] Here is one of mine.

On December 8, 2009, I offered Mass for the Immaculate Conception at St. Margareta, the medieval parish church of Höflein, Austria. I had served there since 2007. For years, starting in 2002 when I became a novice at Klosterneuburg, I painstakingly prepared my homilies in German, drafting them, reviewing them with a native speaker, and preparing a script. After reading the Gospel, I realized I didn't need the text. Dramatically casting the papers aside, I preached freely in German, after seven long, hard years of work. On that day, I finally felt I could say truly that I spoke German. Fourteen years later, on the Feast of the Assumption, I had the opportunity to recall this moment to the same people in the same church.

I chose to learn German because I became a Canon of Klosterneuburg. When I entered, I was already a diocesan priest who had enjoyed a wonderful first assignment in Virginia. Yet I believed that this call to the canonical life was important for myself and for the Church in America, as it was my hope that we would introduce this way of life here (another fulfillment story). Coming to Austria forced me out of my comfort zone and placed me into a state of weakness and powerlessness. It's humiliating to be an adult who cannot make himself understood. Preaching without a script, freely, as myself, was my standard for judging if I did it well. (Recall the above discussion about self-expression.) Did it mean that I spoke beautifully, grammatically flawless German? Of course not. I do not even manage that in English all the time. Yet, I had crossed an important threshold. It brought a deep, enduring joy that has ceaselessly enriched my life.

---

6. Burgis, 163.

IMITATIO CHRISTI

Although "scandals must come" (see Matt. 18:7), we are able to resist negative mimesis. Rather than unconsciously imitating the model-obstacle, who in turn experiences me as a model-obstacle (i.e., double mediation), are we able to find a positive, non-rivalrous model who can inspire thick desires? Girard strongly answers that Christ or anyone who imitates him proposes a safe model. Imitating Christ, Paul urges the Corinthians to imitate him (1 Cor. 4:16), thereby creating "an endless chain of 'good imitation', non-rivalrous imitation, that Christians try to create. The 'saints' are the links of this chain."[7] The Church, therefore, is truly a communion of saints, not just the canonized, but everyone who models Christ.

It begins historically with the life of Jesus. Though distant in time as a memory, the Holy Spirit re-presents Christ, preeminently in the Real Presence of the Blessed Sacrament but also in the sacraments, the liturgy, the proclamation of the Word, works of charity and mercy, the witness of fidelity and sacrificial love in ordinary life, and extraordinary moments of martyrdom. While Church members can scandalize others when they remain under negative mimesis, they can also inspire, comfort, encourage, and strengthen each other when they follow the example of Jesus.

This image of the Church as a communion of saints corresponds closely to the Canadian philosopher Charles Taylor's description of the Church as a "network society, even though of an utterly unparalleled kind, in that the relations are not mediated by any of the historical forms of relatedness: kinship, fealty to a chief, or whatever. It transcends all these, but not into a categorical society based on similarity of members, like citizenship; but rather into a network of ever different relationships of agape."[8] The imitation of Christ is therefore both communal and personal;

---

7. Girard, *Evolution and Conversion*, 160.
8. Charles Taylor, *A Secular Age* (Cambridge, MA: Belknap, 2007), 282.

it is the family of God redeemed from "Adam's family" and invigorated by friendship. Each person must choose to carry the cross, but, unlike Jesus, none should carry it alone. The Church as a community precedes, accompanies, and succeeds every disciple. It shares its wisdom and example even as every disciple enriches the same Church with his or her wisdom and example.

The evangelical demythologization of the world has desacralized or secularized all transcendent models that once existed—namely, gods and heroes.[9] Indeed, even Satan has been naturalized, reduced to the personification of the scapegoat mechanism, which is how Girard interprets Jesus' claim "I saw Satan fall like lightning" (Luke 10:18 RSV-CE).[10] For Girard, this means that Satan is dethroned from the heavens. He is not divine, but a creature, like you or me. Theologically, he is a spiritual being; anthropologically, he represents the scapegoat mechanism's double transference of the victim as diabolical and sacred, the gods and goddesses of archaic religion.

Christ, on the other hand, is safe to imitate because he has revealed the workings of mimesis, the dangers of bad mimesis, and the possibility of peaceful, noncompetitive mimesis. Following Christ is the path of learning to love as Jesus loves in his relationship with his Father.[11] As the perfect image of the Father, Jesus desires to do what his Father desires (John 14:7, 6:38). They practice a positive mimesis (see John 14:9–10). Renouncing rivalry with the one nearest, the neighbor, in favor of effacing oneself, we imitate Christ. By doing this (see John 14:12), one fulfills the New Commandment to love as Jesus loves (John 13:34). And Christ proclaims, "Truly I tell you, just as you did it to one of the least of these who are members of my family, you did it to me"

---

9. Girard, *Battling to the End*, 134.

10. René Girard, *I See Satan Fall Like Lightning*, trans. James G. Williams (Maryknoll, NY: Orbis, 2001), 192.

11. Girard, 13.

(Matt. 25:40).[12] God stands at the right distance, intimate and transcendent simultaneously. But how is this accomplished, that God, dissociated from the sacred, can be at the right distance?

WITHDRAWAL

This peaceful imitation of Christ and the saints has become possible because God, who was once seemingly so close in the violent sacred and thereby apparently justifying it, has withdrawn. God has given us the right distance by which we can imitate him without entering into a rivalry with him. This withdrawal reaches a climax in the Ascension, when the Lord Jesus commissions his disciples to act in his name under the guidance of the Paraclete. Yet already in the virginal conception of Christ, Girard detects hints of the demythologization of the sacred underway as Mary responds with her *fiat* (Luke 1:38): "No relationship of violence exists between those who take part in the virgin birth: the Angel, the Virgin and the Almighty. . . . In fact, all the themes and terms associated with the virgin birth convey to us a perfect submission to the non-violent will of God."[13]

How should we understand submission to the nonviolent will of God? When his disciples asked him to teach them how to pray, Jesus gave them the Lord's Prayer. There one prays, "Thy will be done." The divine will, however, is vastly different from the human will. While we can distinguish between our intellect and our will, there is no such distinction in God, who is utterly simple; complexity is not a sign of divinity. Complex systems break down easily, which for living beings means death. Because God is simple, his word and his will are the same. Thus, any connotations of force are entirely absent from God. God does not impose his will on human beings; he is the source of human freedom.

12. Girard, *Battling to the End*, 133.
13. René Girard, *Things Hidden since the Foundation of the World*, trans. Stephen Bann and Michael Metteer (Stanford, CA: Stanford University Press, 1987), 221.

As we see in the Annunciation, God treats Mary as a partner and friend. He sends a messenger to preserve her freedom; he will not overwhelm her with his majesty. The messenger presents the plan. She replies with questions until satisfied. As if to underscore the reasonableness of God, she substitutes "word" for "will": "Let it be with me according to your word" (Luke 1:38). Her receptivity is not passivity. She lets it happen. It is her choice. There is no hint of force or divine rape as found frequently in Greek mythology.[14]

The child born to Mary, Jesus, the Son of God, is the source of the new knowledge of human violence and the peaceful holy God. The process of revelation reached its apex in the Paschal Mystery, whereupon human perception, not God, changed.[15] Thanks to the divine pedagogy of the cross, human beings must account for their own violence and no longer implicate God in these choices. In this, a new sense of the Second Commandment (Exod. 20:7)—namely, not to misuse the Lord's name—unfolds, because using God's name to justify human violence betrays his holiness. This withdrawal further shows that God is not a product of the scapegoat mechanism's sacralization of the victim, which is directly opposite to withdrawal because it produces the sacred's proximity and promiscuity in human affairs.[16]

Girard corresponds this claim to a passage from Friedrich Hölderlin's poem "Patmos," named after the island where St. John, the seer of the book of Revelation, was exiled.[17]

---

14. Observing that "when Zeus turns into a swan to become Leda's lover we do not think of the crime of bestiality," Girard notes that the aesthetical and poetic treatment of a subject can reveal or conceal real events of scapegoating (in other versions, Zeus rapes Leda) (Girard, *The Scapegoat*, trans. Yvonne Freccero [Baltimore, MD: Johns Hopkins University Press, 1986], 80).

15. Girard, *Battling to the End*, 217–218.

16. Girard, 129.

17. Girard, 121.

Nah ist	Near is,
und schwer zu fassen der Gott.	and difficult to grasp, the God.
Wo aber Gefahr ist, wächst	But where danger threatens,
das Rettende auch.	that which saves from it also grows.

In Girard's view, Hölderlin understood the paradox of human existence under the Gospel. The gods, once so near and easy to grasp (the sacred), have been succeeded by God, who is silent. "The death of the gods"—that is, the disenchantment accomplished by the Gospel—has left the human race in a void and an absence in which it encounters the choice to imitate Christ or perish in a conflagration of human violence, shorn of its sacred veneer: "It is because he is 'difficult to grasp' that this god 'saves' from 'where danger threatens,' in other words, from the time of the corrupted sacred."[18]

Indeed, the silence of God is the condition for this free choice. It is also, however, the cause for the accelerating violence. The recourse to scapegoating is no longer feasible because its cathartic effects are temporary and enfeebled. It has lost its power to create culture (myth, ritual, prohibition, the *katéchon*) since we now know when we are scapegoating. (Or at least, enough people do to make it impossible, as the recent polemics during the COVID-19 pandemic showed: no enduring majority came into existence to successfully blame anyone or any group for the pandemic.) The withdrawal of God culminates in Christ's Ascension: he will speak no more; eyes will no longer see him. He is now a model with whom one cannot engage in a mimetic rivalry because of his transcendence. At the same time, Christ

---

18. Girard, 122.

remains mystically present in the Church and to the world as he promised: "I am with you always, to the end of the age" (Matt. 28:20b). He authorizes his disciples to imitate him in relationships of charity rather than in reciprocity of escalating violence (see Matt. 28:19–20a).

Acting like Christ means becoming like him, a son or daughter of God: "But to all who received him, who believed in his name, he gave power to become children of God, who were born, not of blood or of the will of the flesh or of the will of man, but of God" (John 1:12–13). The "bread of angels"—the passive, silent, powerless Host—grounds us in the fundamental truth of our nature as creatures. Yet where the Head has gone in glory, the Body follows in hope. In the ascended yet present Christ, humanity has its perfect model.

THE RIGHT DISTANCE

The withdrawal of God from the world—the natural-cultural order produced by the violent sacred—and the withdrawal of the ascended Christ are the conditions of possibility for positive mimesis. These establish an external mediation (Celebristan) that gives human beings a nonviolent model with whom they cannot compete. At the foot washing, Jesus gave a New Commandment to love as he loved us (John 13:34). His love for us is the standard by which we should love others. Since Jesus is the mediator who is present in our neighbor and present to God, he places humanity at the right distance to one another: "He is the one that is most outside yet also most inside common humanity. He is *the most divine and the most human.*"[19]

Girard sees this paradox in Augustine's statement, "You were more inward than the most inward place of my heart and loftier than the highest" (*Deus interior intimo meo et superior summo*

---

19. Girard, 50. Emphasis in the original.

meo).[20] In other words, God is closer to us than we are to ourselves, and yet at the same time utterly transcendent. God therefore can no longer be confused with the violent sacred (and its gods), for God is no longer on this earth; yet, at the same time, God is present in the neighbor, who is not the rival to imitate, but the one to love as Christ has loved us, and as one whom Christ loves through us. Imitating Christ and the saints excludes rivalry with others because the latter necessarily reverts to violence.[21]

IDENTIFICATION

Girard contrasts the right distance to the danger of "indifferentiation," which refers to the elimination of differences in the face of mimetic rivalry.[22] Differences order human relationships to mitigate mimetic desires. They arise from the first difference established in the original scapegoating event, which opposes the scapegoat to the community, the guilty to the innocent, the bad to the good. Societies depend on differences between individuals and groups to maintain peace. Instantiations of the *katéchon* maintain these differences to manage mimetic desire (e.g., religion consecrates persons; ritual marks boundaries; and prohibitions forbid conduct, objects, desires, etc.). The maintenance of differences therefore is a critical function in any society. The diminution of differences and the rise of indifferentiation heralds a mimetic crisis. Consequently, indifferentiation reduces a group from ordered diversity and structured differences to a state of equality, identity, and uniformity.

Christ, however, transforms this dangerous process of differentiation from its context of violent expulsion (scapegoat mechanism) to a new context of peaceful reconciliation. As the innocent

---

20. Augustine, *Confessions* 3.6, trans. F.J. Sheed (Park Ridge, IL: Word on Fire Classics, 2017), 50.
21. Girard, *Battling to the End*, 129.
22. Girard, 133.

one, he establishes a new state of indifferentiation or identity. Against the innocent one is the entire human race, whose mimetic desire tends toward violence. Rather than condemning the human race as different from him, however, Christ, by his Incarnation, Baptism, and Paschal Mystery, underscores at every step his total identification with the human race: "For our sake [God] made [Christ] to be sin who knew no sin, so that in him we might become the righteousness of God" (2 Cor. 5:21). Jesus breaks down the walls that divide because the new unity does not require a victim or a scapegoat, but conversion.

Paul writes to the Colossians, "You have stripped off the old self with its practices and have clothed yourselves with the new self, which is being renewed in knowledge according to the image of its creator. In that renewal there is no longer Greek and Jew, circumcised and uncircumcised, barbarian, Scythian, slave and free; but Christ is all and in all!" (Col. 3:9–11). Paul is explaining the consequence of Baptism: it is a new life that sets one on a journey to grow in resemblance to the Creator. Then he explains the ramifications of Christ's identification with everyone ("all in all"). Earlier differences are no longer relevant. Whether these differences were God-ordained, such as the distinction between Jew and Greek (non-Jewish nations), circumcised (in the covenants of Abraham and Sinai) and uncircumcised (outside), or male and female (Gen. 1:27), or arose out of mimetic processes that created human cultures (e.g., foreigner or Scythian, and their institutions, such as slave and free), they have all been set aside and relativized. Christ confers a new dignity of humanity by his identification with the baptized, and further, by the open invitation to all human beings to be baptized. The radical implications of this new equality were often rightly perceived by defenders of various sacred orders as dangerously revolutionary.

Yet, this does not cause a new mimetic crisis of indifferentiation, but rather establishes a safe mimesis by which we can imitate Jesus, who imitates his Father in peace rather than succumbing to mimetic rivalry. God the Son has never tried to kill his Father as the gods of mythology often do. He exists in perfect mimesis with his eternal Father, of whom he is the perfect image (Col. 1:15). Thus, the peaceful mimesis of God comes to the human race through the work of the Holy Trinity. There is no coercion or force in God. God the Father does not impose the plan of salvation on his Son, as it has sometimes been supposed. The mystery of redemption is a common work of the Father, Son, and Spirit—a mighty and amazing deed carried out through the full decision of each of the three persons.

As the vindicated scapegoat, Christ therefore possessed the prerogative to establish a new difference between himself and humanity as that of the innocent one to the guilty. Films and novels display this form of logic in which the victim (or someone else in his or her name) wreaks vengeance on the guilty for their crimes. Instead, however, the risen Christ forgives to remove real guilt and welcomes everyone to imitate him in his relationship with the Father. This is the coming of the kingdom in which positive identification with others results in justice, peace, and joy (see Rom. 14:17). In Christ and through the Holy Spirit, the disordered relationships caused by original sin may now be restored to righteousness and holiness because man stands at the right distance to God and to one another.

CONCLUSION

"I Came to Cast Fire"

Girard was a master of titles. He often chose alluring Scripture passages to draw the reader into his wrestling with that "single, extremely dense insight." The title of this book is my homage to him. And if I have told this story well, then I hope that you have caught on fire with the same love for God that Girard's mimetic theory did for me. When I beheld the cover of *I See Satan Fall Like Lightning*, I could not have imagined how much that book would change my life. In hindsight, more than twenty years later, I can see the significance of the cover design. At the center of the cover is Parmigianino's *The Conversion of Saint Paul*.

Without saying it out loud, I think it is right to say that Girard's message to his reader is conversion, not only personally but also globally. Without this conversion, mimetic desire will consume the earth. As it must, such a conversion begins with each one of us, as it did with Saul the persecutor who became Paul the penitent sinner. Love empowers us to face the truth that we are all like Saul and we need to become like Paul. In our own conversions, we will also discover the immense gift of mimetic theory, whose future is very bright because of its capacity to look at the world with a new perspective.

Here's one that is near and dear to me. Girard gives us tools for thinking about history anew, and Parmigianino's painting of St. Paul helps me tell this story. Displayed since 1912 in the famous Kunsthistorisches Museum (Art History Museum) in Vienna, the painting is a short distance from my home at my abbey in Klosterneuburg. Situated on a large plaza at the heart of which is the colossal monument of Maria Theresa, enthroned as empress, serenely gazing upon the Heldenplatz (Heroes' Plaza) and the Hofburg (Imperial Palace) across the street, the Art History Museum and its twin, the Natural History Museum, underscore the prominence of history as an artistic style as well as a scientific discipline in the late nineteenth century. History, as we have seen, when done in the pursuit of the truth, overturns myth and rehabilitates the victim. But it can also be misused to victimize anew.

With the decision to tear down the city walls that had protected *Das schöne Wien* ("Beautiful Vienna") from the two Ottoman sieges of the "Golden Apple," as the Turks called the city, in 1529 and 1683, opportunities arose for a new urban landscape. Consequently, a crowded cavalcade of historicist monuments appeared along the Ringstraße (Ring Road), including the neo-Gothic city hall, the neo-Classical parliament, the neo-Renaissance state opera house, and the neo-Romanesque barracks. Historicist architects and artists imitated earlier styles from Europe and beyond, sometimes eclectically mixing them as never before (hence the affix *neo-*, "new"). The movement reflected the growing globalization of the world through the conquest of time and space by science and technology, and of peoples and places by empire.

As the seat of the Habsburg dynasty for many centuries until the end of monarchy more than a century ago in 1918, Vienna symbolizes well the Christian predicament. The city overflows with the artifacts of an imperial past. Yet for all the splendor of its magnificent churches, abbeys, and ecclesiastical institutions, the faith is struggling. Why? Because "a colonized society"—in this case the Catholic Church—"inevitably withers away, it becomes cowardly, second-rate, negligible."[1] Let me explain. In Austria,

---

1. Ewa Thompson, "Stefan Żeromski's *Ashes* as a Postcolonial Narrative," *Historyka: Studia metodologiczne* 42, English-German version (2012): 77–95, at 93.

Catholics, among whom there are many immigrants, bear this strange double burden of the imperial past, which cannot be easily distinguished from the Catholic faith, and the hostility to that same faith because of the weight of this history. The same can be said for Catholics throughout the West and beyond. Laboring under this burden, we are tempted to succumb to a mimetically induced inferiority complex vis-à-vis the dominant culture (the colonizer) despite its obvious pathologies.

Although the instrumentalization of the crimes and errors of the Christian past is too alluring to those who wish to deflect attention from those of the present, Girard makes it possible to escape this cycle of accusation and victimization. We can lay aside our predictable defensive reaction to these attacks when we learn the truth of the Paraclete: the history of the Church is more nuanced and more redeemable than the simplified, black and white, good versus bad, Manichean version that is repeated today in classrooms and on podcasts. Trashing the past to justify the present is a disease of the mind because it comes from the scapegoat mechanism's duplicitous division between the good and the evil. Jesus admonished us to avoid judging others because, as the vindicated victim, he is the only one who is authorized to do so.

Our experience of this double colonization—we were once the good guys, now we are the bad guys—can be a grace. It can be part of the plan of the Paraclete to give us a chance to think about all of this anew. Taking inspiration from the Colombian philosopher Nicolás Gómez Dávila's aphorism #2,801—"After the experience of an age that is practically devoid of religion, Christianity learns to write the history of paganism with respect and sympathy"[2]—we can write a new history of religion (in other words, of humanity) with generosity and sympathy, so that the scapegoat's

---

2. "Después de experimentar en qué consiste una época prácticamente sin religión, el cristianismo aprende a escribir la historia del paganismo con respeto y con simpatía" (#2801), Nicolás Gómez Dávila, *Escolios a un texto implícito: Selección* (Bogotá: Villegas Editores, 2001), 449.

dichotomy between the good and the bad is returned to the one place where it belongs: our divided hearts.[3]

Returning to the enchanting cover, we see the moment of Saul's crisis of conscience (Acts 9:1–9). Having witnessed the martyrdom of St. Stephen, to which he later admitted after his conversion that he consented (Acts 22:20), he set out to arrest the followers of the Way in Damascus. In Parmigianino's painting, Saul looks up to the heavens, whereas the horse looks at us. The cover is a *décollage*, a technique in which parts of the original are torn away to produce something new. In this case, the image lacks the background—the heavens, Damascus, the caravan, and the wild animals. In this void, between author and title, Saul reacts to the flash of light and to the question, "Saul, Saul, why do you persecute me?" The painting captures Saul asking, "Who are you, Lord?" Who is this Lord? "I am Jesus, whom you are persecuting," he answers, implicitly declaring that Saul is persecuting God.

The juxtaposition of the decontextualized image and the title connects the dethroning of Satan in St. Luke's Gospel to the conversion of Saul in St. Luke's Acts. Jesus commands Saul to go to the city, where he will find out what he must do. By removing Damascus from the cover, the city to which Jesus refers can be any city, even the first city. (Recall that for Girard, the city represents the culture that emerges from the scapegoat mechanism.) Saul embodies the transition from the sacred (the earthly city of Cain and his descendants, which includes us) to the holy (the heavenly Jerusalem), from an alliance with violence, hiding under clever justifications and sophisticated rationalizations—all of which are modern versions of myth—to its truthful recognition and renunciation.

While both fall—Satan from heaven, and Saul from his horse—the symmetry ends there because their outcomes are

---

3. Joseph Julián González and Monique González have made just such an attempt in their fascinating account of the Mesoamerican cultural background to the mass conversion to Christianity of indigenous peoples after the apparition at Guadalupe in *Guadalupe and the Flower World Prophecy: How God Prepared the Americas for Conversion Before the Lady Appeared* (Manchester, NH: Sophia Institute, 2023).

radically different. As we have seen, Girard interprets Jesus' statement about Satan to be speaking about Satan as a creature, no longer godlike. Once the secret producer and director of the scapegoat mechanism, Satan's fraudulence is now revealed: he is the scandal and the accusing mob; he is the victim in the double transference who becomes the god (the sacred) and founds the city. After the Resurrection, Satan's deception no longer has the power to create because Jesus has revealed the truth: we know that the scapegoat is never to blame for the crisis. As the father of lies who is a murderer from the beginning (John 8:44), Satan can only destroy.

Falling from his steed, Saul the persecutor becomes Paul the oft-persecuted and finally martyred Apostle. Choosing to imitate Christ in his patience and truth-telling, Paul not only left behind a model to emulate (1 Cor. 11:1) but a theological legacy that ceaselessly bears abundant fruit. The conversion of Saul, therefore, is not only a personal grace, but as it is decontextualized on the cover without a specific reference to time and place, it serves likewise as a story for every person. By placing ourselves between the author and the title, we, too, may experience a dramatic upheaval in our worldview, a fall from a horse, or perhaps more accurately, a death to the mimetically driven delusions of the Romantic self, and a resurrection to connection, communion, and completion—just as Girard himself underwent in his conversion, spending his life unraveling that "single, extremely dense insight."

But there is still more. In 1527, Parmigianino finished his painting in Bologna just a few months after fleeing the sack of Rome. The mutinous imperial army of Charles V, the universal Habsburg emperor, unleashed its greedy and lustful vengeance on the populace: half was murdered, and the rest violated, raped, and robbed. Some interpreted the sack as an act of divine punishment against the corrupt papacy. The Church was left adrift in the aftermath of the sack. The emperor ascended in power vis-à-vis the papacy, the chances for a reconciliation between reformers and the Church rapidly diminished, and the Italian peninsula and its people became the plaything of foreign dynastic powers, ensnared in their mimetic rivalries for four centuries. Lastly, for a long time, many credited Nicolò dell'Abate, a founder of the French Mannerist School of Fontainebleau, as the painter of *The Conversion of Saint Paul*. As the result of careful recent historical research, however, the truth has vindicated Parmigianino, the "little Parmesan," Girolamo Francesco Maria Mazzola, as its real painter. Another victory for the Paraclete, who leads us into truth.

For more than twenty years, mimetic theory has helped me to interpret the mimetic rivalries, social contagions, and scapegoating (e.g., September 11 and the wars that followed, the mimetic mutations of the sexual revolution, cancel culture, the Trump phenomenon, the pandemic, and numerous intra-ecclesial conflicts and scandals) that engulf our world. Girard has indeed discovered something of immense value. He changed my life. He gave me knowledge that can make the world a better place. With his insight, it is possible to cultivate a life in which mimetic rivalry can be opposed with truth, wisdom, and charity. I hope that this book has succeeded in its modest aim to entice you to read Girard. If so, then like the woman at the well, who, overjoyed about Jesus, ran to her fellow Samaritans, I too will not be needed, because you have gone to Girard directly. Like her, I simply fade away.

But I am not the only one. Girard does the same. His thoughts are not his. They are from Jesus. Read Girard and discover Jesus anew. The world needs courageous people who can love their enemies because they know that human beings are not the enemy; mimesis gone awry is. We will be able to imitate Christ in his forbearing love for us. The fire he casts does not destroy us; it purifies us of our fears of not getting what we want. Be free, therefore, because victory is assured. It belongs to him alone, and we are his.

Glossary

archaic religion: See *sacred*.

contagion (also social or mimetic contagion): Appealing to the metaphor of plague or contagion, Girard uses these related terms to refer to the communal nature of mimetic conflicts. Interpersonal mimetic rivalries are subsumed into larger communal mimetic rivalries. Girard uses a number of terms to describe the intensification of mimetic rivalry on a communal level, including "mimetic crisis," "snowballing," "escalation to the extremes," and "polarization." The invisible spread of mimetic rivalries mirrors the invisible spread of bacterial or viral contagion. Girard adds "social" or "mimetic" to distinguish it from a purely biological plague. He does, however, see that two phenomena often overlap with each other. A biological plague intensifies social or mimetic contagion in terms of the hunt for scapegoats—those responsible for the crisis—as the COVID-19 pandemic demonstrated.

culture: Girard uses this term to refer to the institutions and practices that emerge from the scapegoat mechanism. The earliest foundations for culture are myth, prohibition, and ritual. The list is not intended to be exhaustive. Under the pressure of mimesis, cultures add new forms of organization and institutions (e.g., sacred kingship), all of which are subsumed under the *katéchon*. These institutions and practices restrain violence, and modern innovations try to diffuse and harness mimetic desire.

desire: Derived from the Latin *desiderare* (to long for someone or something that is absent), this term consists of *de-* (from) and *-sidus* (star). Girard contrasts appetites (*appétits*, needs) and desires (*désirs*, wants). Needs are grounded in biology, but wants in other human beings—that is, in models whose own wants excite desire. Mimesis influences both needs and wants because it is through models (examples of desires) that human beings discover what they desire.

double mediation: In a mimetic relationship, both the subject/person and the model/other/mediator mediate desire to each other. When the model detects the initial interest of the subject's desire for the model's object, the subject then also becomes a model for the model. Their desires become mutually reinforcing, bringing a mimetic rivalry into existence.

double transference/transformation: This refers to the effect of the scapegoat mechanism on the victim/sacrifice. First, in the mimetic crisis, the crowd naïvely judges the victim to be the diabolical source of their division and frustration, which causes them to expel the victim. After the cathartic effect of the expulsion, the crowd also attributes a supernatural power to the victim as the source of their reconciliation and peace. The second movement renders the victim-as-demon into victim-as-sacred. Girard points to evidence of this double transference/transformation in mythology, where the gods appear to embody both sides (e.g., Dionysius), and in the New Testament anthropological interpretation of Satan.

dramatic theology: A theological framework that was developed by the Innsbruck theologian Raymund Schwager, SJ, in tandem with Girard's mimetic theory. Schwager advanced insights similar to Girard before they met. Their fruitful partnership enriched both mimetic theory and dramatic theology. Providing an interpretative center that biblical exegesis and theology lack, dramatic theology seeks to bring together biblical and dogmatic theology, explaining the Chalcedonian dogma of Jesus (true God and true man) in light of the insights of mimetic theory, the scapegoat mechanism, the Paschal Mystery, and the evangelical subversion of the sacred.

escalation to the extremes: This is a term from Girard's reflection on the Prussian military theorist Carl von Clausewitz's *On War* in *Battling to the End*. Girard employs escalation to the extremes (*das Streben nach dem Äußersten*) as another way of referring to mimesis and its effects. On an interpersonal level, this refers to the stages in mimetic rivalry that can end in murder, but often are subsumed into other communal conflicts, a social or mimetic contagion. In this case, polarization causes the community to achieve an all-against-one unity that ends in the scapegoat mechanism, in which the personal and communal conflicts are placed upon the scapegoat, who bears these negative emotions away.

expulsion of the victim: This is another of Girard's expressions for the scapegoat mechanism.

external mediation: The structure of triangular desire is inherent in human relationships. The key variable for whether such mimetic desire will lead to peaceful imitation or violent conflict is distance, in a social rather than a spatial sense. Sufficient distance prevents the escalation to the extremes because it places the subject/person and his model/other/mediator far enough apart to make conflict unlikely. Girard calls this "external mediation," whereas its opposite, "internal mediation," refers to too little distance, which makes rivalry and violence possible, if not likely. Luke Burgis names external mediation "Celebristan" and internal mediation "Freshmanistan."

founding murder: For Girard, scapegoating first took the form of human sacrifice as the original lynching event, which he calls the "founding murder." Through the expulsion of the scapegoat, a new culture comes into existence.

holy: While the sacred refers to that which results from the scapegoat mechanism, the "holy" is that which emerges from within the sacred—concisely put, human culture—as the revelation of the nonviolent, true God, through the Paschal Mystery. The confusion of the sacred and the holy, therefore, ends with the Resurrection of Jesus and the mission of the Paraclete, even if this effect works over millennia in history.

imitation: See *mimesis*.

innocent victim: Contrary to the claims of the scapegoating community as reported in their myth that the scapegoat is guilty, Girard argues that the scapegoat is innocent. When he calls the scapegoat an innocent victim, he is merely affirming that the scapegoat is no more responsible for the mimetic crisis than any other member of the community. He is not implying an ontological or moral innocence, which belongs alone to Christ.

internal mediation: See *external mediation*.

katéchon: This refers to "a restraining force" (see 2 Thess. 2:6–7). In Girard's terms, the *katéchon* uses limited violence to control the unlimited violence that comes from mimetic rivalry. Beginning with the scapegoat mechanism, the *katéchon* has subsequently evolved into a variety of institutions, practices, and ideas that seek to protect human beings from mimetic rivalry over the long term. The Gospel's announcement of the innocence of the victim created a unique environment to which the *katéchon* adapted, giving rise to modernity.

méconnaissance: The revelation of the scapegoat mechanism laid bare the manner in which myth concealed the truth about what was really going on; that is to say, the New Testament exposed the lie behind myth, which told the story of the original scapegoating event from the perspective of the persecuting community. The actual murder of the innocent victim is misapprehended: the victim is held to be both the cause of the mimetic crisis as well as its resolution. Girard argues that the New Testament uses the term Satan on an anthropological level to explain this double transference as cause and solution to the crisis.

mediation: This refers to the relationship between the subject/person and the model/other/mediator in which desires are exchanged by imitation or mimesis. Initially, the subject/person desires an object of the model/other/mediator. The desirability of the object, however, does not lie in itself but in the model/other/mediator. Once the model/other/mediator detects the interests of the subject/person, then the latter becomes a model for the former, thus initiating double mediation. The peaceful or violent outcome of this mediation depends on whether the mediation is internal or external.

mediator: The mediator is the one whom the subject/person imitates. Although Girard uses "model," "other," and "mediator" interchangeably, mediation, double mediation, external mediation, and internal mediation relate to the role of the mediator.

metaphysical poverty: Underneath Girard's reflection on mimetic desire is his claim that human beings as contingent beings who live and die, grow and wither, increase and decrease perceive themselves as poor in being. Hence, Cynthia L. Haven has gathered Girard's essential texts under the title *All Desire Is a Desire for Being*. Human beings do not create themselves, and those who seem to be overflowing with being attract us. Drawn to these models, we want to acquire their being by wanting what they have, so that we can become more like them; indeed, we can even *become* them. Advertising practitioners use this knowledge to fashion campaigns to sell goods and services. They associate their consumable objects with qualities of health, success, and fame through their strategic choice of models from athletics, Hollywood, the entertainment industry, etc.

mimesis: Girard describes human desire as "mimetic" because he has observed a link between what people want and who else wants it. *Mimesis* is the Greek word that we know in English as "imitation" (from the Latin *imitatio*).

mimetic crisis: The accumulation of interpersonal mimetic rivalries in a community becomes a generalized social contagion that threatens to engulf the community in boundless violence. If the community should survive, it will need to release its mimetic contagion through the scapegoat mechanism.

mimetic desire: This refers to imitating the desire of another human being. Girard argues that human desire exhibits a powerfully mimetic character. I want what another has because I perceive the other as wealthy in being where I suffer from metaphysical poverty. Because this desire operates from the earliest moments of human life in childhood, we are long since under its sway before we can learn to control it. This mimetic or imitative desire confers great benefits to the human race, but at the price of boundless violence.

mimetic doubles: This concept is related to double mediation. In the case of internal mediation, it refers specifically to the process of an increasing loss of difference between the subject/person and the model/other/mediator. Unless a communal conflict subsumes the interpersonal mimetic rivalry, one expects to see the two persons resemble each other increasingly through the reciprocity of their actions: one curse calls forth another, one blow another. Girard argues that when the conflict has reached this level, the attention of the object fades away, replaced with the desire to overcome the opponent.

mimetic rivalry: As the subject/person and the model/other/mediator scandalize each other through double mediation, the two parties grow more hostile to each other. This rivalry can escalate to the extremes of violence unless the conflict shifts to a communal level, feeding a social contagion or mimetic crisis. If a community is to avoid unbounded violence, it follows a process of polarization that brings about a unity of all against one to spring the scapegoat mechanism, the original *katéchon*. Humanity has continued to devise new forms of the *katéchon* to contain and limit violence as well as to harness mimetic desire.

mimetism: Girard occasionally uses this term to refer to mimesis in its various aspects.

misapprehension: See *méconnaissance*.

model: The model is the one whom the subject/person imitates. Girard uses "model," "other," and "mediator" interchangeably.

myth: Referring to stories about the origins of the divine, natural, and social worlds and of practices such as ritual, sacrifice, and taboos, Girard explains that myths misapprehend (see *méconnaissance*) the truth about the scapegoat mechanism. Myth "mutes" the cry of the innocent victim and furnishes the community with a story that justifies its behavior.

object: See *triangular desire*.

other: The other is the one whom the subject/person imitates. Girard uses "model," "other," and "mediator" interchangeably.

Paraclete: This term, derived from the Gospel of John, is one of the titles of the Holy Spirit. Girard places immense importance on the role of the Holy Spirit in history as the Paraclete because in its original judicial context it means "attorney for the defense." In the face of Satan's accusation, the Paraclete declares that the scapegoat is in fact an innocent victim of mob violence. The lie of the myth is overturned through the proclamation of the truth in the Gospel, which begins with the Resurrection of Jesus. After Pentecost, the Holy Spirit works in the world to bring this message everywhere through the Church as a public witness and through the mysterious operation of grace in human hearts.

person: Girard uses this term interchangeably with "subject" in the context of explaining the triangular relationship of mimetic desire.

plague: See *contagion*.

polarization: This refers to the process by which the community arrives at the candidate for scapegoating. Girard argues that mimetic rivalry exhibits a snowballing effect. As interpersonal conflicts are subsumed into larger communal conflicts, the community eventually achieves a unity of all against one, which presages the expulsion of the victim.

prohibition: Arising out of the scapegoat mechanism along with ritual and myth, the new cultural order sanctifies rules of conduct—namely, taboos and prohibitions—to forbid those behaviors that cause mimetic rivalries. In this lies the origins of law, the judiciary, and law enforcement. Inasmuch as mimetic desire naturally focuses on the neighbor and his possessions, prohibitions interrupt this desire by making the neighbor and his possessions too distant and unapproachable, at least in a moral sense. Yet prohibitions alone, though directed to peace, are inadequate for achieving this end. As Paul's analysis of the Law demonstrates, prohibitions, too, can aggravate and excite desire. Their negative sense is unsatisfying.

reciprocity: See *double mediation* and *mimetic doubles*.

ritual: Along with myth and prohibition, ritual is one of the three institutions of culture, and issues forth from the successful functioning of the scapegoat mechanism. The ritual reenactment of the original scapegoating event in sacrifice, Girard argues, formed humanity. It may even have furnished the context in which the first symbol arose.

Romantic lie: This phrase derives from Girard's first book, *Mensonge romantique et vérité romanesque*, literally rendered in English as "Romantic Lies and Novelistic Truth" (later translated as *Deceit, Desire, and the Novel*). His title in French explains what is at stake: modernity is founded on the Romantic lie that human beings determine their desires autonomously and freely. The novelistic truth contradicts this claim, stating that mimetic desire more powerfully influences desire than reason or will. Girard recognizes that while these books were structurally the same as other novels, their handling of mimesis is different: the authors either passively reflect on mediated or mimetic desire, or they have the courage to reveal its influence. He detects the cycle of death and resurrection for those who admit the power of mimesis, because that power humiliates the modern autonomous self, disclosing it to be dependent and poor, which is both true and liberating. Girard uses the same argument when he contrasts the structurally similar stories of scapegoating in mythology and the Gospels. Their difference emerges clearly in their divergent interpretation of the guilt of the victim: myths side with the community, and the Gospels side with the victim.

sacred: Girard borrowed the concept of "the sacred" from Émile Durkheim, but he took it in his own direction by contrasting the sacred with the holy. "The sacred" refers to that which results from the scapegoat mechanism, whereas "the holy" refers to that which emerges from within the sacred as the revelation of the nonviolent, true God, through the Paschal Mystery. The sacred is the reverse side of violence: it comes from the violence of the scapegoat mechanism. It refers to the god or goddess that the double transference produces as well as the foundational elements of culture: myth, prohibition, and ritual. The sacred, therefore, is often synonymous with culture (*cult*) and politics (*polis*, "city") because human societies from the earliest stages are sacrificial communities. Girard also refers to the sacred as "archaic religion."

sacrifice: In Girard's earlier writings, this refers exclusively to the ritual repetition of the original scapegoating event upon which a culture is founded. In *Things Hidden since the Foundation of the World*, Girard sometimes contrasts sacrificial to non-sacrificial Christianity—the former being still under the influence of mimetism (the sacred), the latter no longer. Girard, it should be noted, later repudiated this distinction. Under the influence of Raymund Schwager, he embraced Christ's reinterpretation of sacrifice as self-offering as a positive alternative to sacrifice as a scapegoat.

Satan: Girard argues the New Testament's use of the term "Satan," which means the "prosecutor" or "accuser" in Hebrew, can be understood on an anthropological level to refer to the scapegoat mechanism. Satan is both the mimetic crisis and the victim who solves it through expulsion; hence, "Satan expels Satan" (see Mark 3:23). Moreover, when Jesus says that he "saw Satan fall like lightning" (Luke 10:18 RSV-CE), Girard interprets this passage to mean that Satan has been desacralized; that is, the sacred, which comes from the scapegoat mechanism, is now seen to be false and not of God. His falling to earth therefore refers to the fact that Satan no longer makes victims gods (the sacred). Thanks to the Paschal Mystery, Satan is dethroned, but not without power as long as mimesis can go awry and unbounded violence threatens. This anthropological reading is not meant to exclude the reality of Satan as a spiritual being.

scandal: Girard employs the biblical terms "scandal"/"scandalize" (*skandalon/skandalizein*) to describe the obstacles over which people stumble (the literal sense of "scandal" in Greek). In double mediation, both the subject/person and the model/other/mediator scandalize each other because each becomes the obstacle to the other's desire being reached. Scandals simultaneously fascinate and repulse, eliciting reciprocity and the escalation to the extremes.

scapegoat: This term, borrowed from the Jewish ritual of expelling the goat into the desert on the Day of Atonement, refers to the one killed in the scapegoat mechanism. See also *expulsion of the victim, innocent victim,* and *victim*.

scapegoating: This refers to the escalating to the extremes or polarization of a group during a social contagion into an all-against-one unity that ends in the murder or expulsion of the victim or the scapegoat. Through this act, the community is released of its tension and stress due to its interpersonal and communal mimetic conflicts by venting them all upon the victim. Girard also calls these events "mob violence" or "lynching." Scapegoating first took the form of human sacrifice as (1) the original lynching event and then (2) the subsequent ritual repetition. The original event he calls the "scapegoat mechanism," while its ritual repetition is generally called "sacrifice."

scapegoat mechanism: In this phrase, Girard combines the act of scapegoating/expulsion with the term "mechanism" to underscore his claim that once the right conditions are met, then the event occurs. If those conditions are not met, then it does not occur, and the mimetic crisis carries on. If the conditions are met, then the community experiences a wondrous reconciliation, and the victim undergoes a double transference. Moreover, if the scapegoating event is to be successful, the scapegoating must remain hidden. The crowd misapprehends what really went on; that is, they believe the innocent victim to be guilty, confessing him or her as a new divinity, giving rise to a new culture (myth, ritual, and prohibition).

single victim mechanism: See *scapegoat mechanism*.

snowballing: As a snowball rolls down a hill, it grows in size as it absorbs more snow. By this metaphor, Girard contends that interpersonal mimetic rivalries tend to be subsumed by communal rivalries. Eventually, through this process of polarization, all other rivalries fall away until the community reaches the all-against-one unity of the scapegoat mechanism.

subject: Girard uses this term interchangeably with "person" in the context of explaining the triangular relationship of mimetic desire.

triangular desire: This term—derived from Girard's first major work, *Deceit, Desire, and the Novel*—refers to the structure of mimesis. Although mimesis is triangular, consisting of (x) the person/subject, (y) the model/other/mediator, and (z) the object, its geometry is not a triangle; rather, it is something more like a sequence, at least at the beginning. For the subject, the model conveys desirability on the object. I want the object because the model wants it.

unbounded violence: Human violence differs from other animals because it overwhelms the usual constraints on violence in the animal kingdom (e.g., instincts, dominance hierarchies, etc.). Girard argues that mimetic desire unleashes the possibility of unbounded human violence that, left unchecked, consumes the community. He hypothesizes that those human communities that did not stumble upon the scapegoat mechanism, which relieved the community of its conflicts by expelling the victim, destroyed themselves.

victim: This term derives from the Latin for a "sacrifice" or "offering"; see *scapegoat*.

victim mechanism: See *scapegoat mechanism*.

violence: While Girard does not deny that violence has other causes, as it does in the animal kingdom, he argues that human violence is especially colored by mimetic desire. Mimetic desire broke through the bonds that contain or limit violence in the animal world, including instincts and dominance hierarchies. The danger of unbounded human violence, fueled by mimetic rivalries that escalate to mimetic crises, required a new corrective mechanism, the scapegoat mechanism, to relieve the crisis and to avoid it in the future; see *katéchon*.

violent sacred: Abbreviated from the title of *Violence and the Sacred*, it can be understood as a summary of the power of violence to create culture through the scapegoat mechanism. It also refers to the double transference of the victim, who through violent expulsion becomes a new divinity ("the sacred"). It is also equivalent to Girard's anthropological interpretation of the role of Satan in the New Testament.

Itineraries for Further Reading

For the most mature summary of mimetic theory, read *I See Satan Fall Like Lightning*. Enriched with his earlier exegetical work as well as with important contributions to his vision of history, this is the best place to start for those who want to strengthen their overview of Girard's work.

For those interested in the life of René Girard, see Cynthia L. Haven's much acclaimed biography, *Evolution of Desire: A Life of René Girard*. Much cited in chapter 1, this biography weaves together Girard's life and texts, providing invaluable insights in the development of mimetic theory.

For overviews of mimetic theory from other authors, see the comprehensive *René Girard's Mimetic Theory* by Wolfgang Palaver, a collaborator of Girard's and Schwager's from Innsbruck. Grant Kaplan's more recent *René Girard, Unlikely Apologist* gives a fascinating exposition of the theological trajectories of mimetic theory. Still valuable are the older introductions to Girard from Michael Kirwan, SJ, *Discovering Girard* and *Girard and Theology*.

For his most mature summary of his vision of history, read *Battling to the End*. In his final major work, a conversation with Benoît Chantre, Girard presents his vision of history through the theme of the Franco-German rivalry. Girard interprets Clausewitz's *On War* and Friedrich Hölderlin's poem "Patmos" through the lens of mimetic theory. He also describes the rivalry between the papacy and the empire, his idea of Europe, and the chances and challenges that face humanity.

For key milestones in the evolution of Girard's mimetic theory, chronologically start with *Deceit, Desire, and the Novel*, then read *Violence and the Sacred*, *Things Hidden since the Foundation of the World*, *The Scapegoat*, *I See Satan Fall Like Lightning*, *Evolution and Conversion*, and, finally, *Battling to the End*.

For those looking for a guided tour of selected writings of Girard, read *All Desire Is a Desire for Being*, edited by Cynthia L. Haven, and *The Girard Reader*, edited by James G. Williams.

For those interested in Girard as a literary critic, there are numerous articles and studies to consider. The first important contribution to mimetic theory is *Deceit, Desire, and the Novel*. Major studies include his early work on Dostoevsky, *Resurrection from the Underground*; *"To double business bound,"* consisting of literary studies and an interview; further studies on myth, persecution, and biblical texts in *The Scapegoat*; his foray into Shakespearean studies, *A Theater of Envy*; his essays on Sophocles' masterpiece, *Oedipus Unbound*; and *Mimesis and Theory*, with twenty of his uncollected essays on literature and criticism gathered together.

For those interested in examples of Girard's exegetical research, a good place to start is *The Scapegoat*, which contains a number of case studies. Girard applies mimetic theory in *Job:*

The Victim of His People. *I See Satan Fall Like Lightning* also has examples.

For those who enjoy reading Girard's insights in a conversational format, read *Things Hidden since the Foundation of the World*. This is his major work after *Violence and the Sacred*. He also published the conversational texts *When These Things Begin* and *The One By Whom Scandal Comes*. See also *Conversations with René Girard: Prophet of Envy*, edited by Cynthia L. Haven, and *The World of René Girard: Interview*s, edited by Nadine Dormoy and translated by William A. Johnsen.

For those interested in the dramatic theology of the Jesuit theologian Raymund Schwager, read *Jesus in the Drama of Salvation*, his mature presentation of the doctrine of salvation enriched by mimetic theory. Schwager at the same time also prepared a novella in which he retells the life of Jesus in a five-part drama, *Jesus of Nazareth*. Schwager gives a comprehensive exposition of mimetic theory in biblical exegesis in his earlier work, *Must There Be Scapegoats?*

For those interested in a contemporary exposition on mimetic desire, read *Wanting*. Cited throughout this work, Luke Burgis offers numerous examples from business and entrepreneurship to demonstrate the strength of mimetic theory as a tool for figuring out what we want. He offers practical advice to discover one's motivation and to reorient one's desires away from rivalry and toward constructive and contributory mimesis.

Girard's Works in English

Girard, René. *Anorexia and Mimetic Desire.* Translated by Mark R. Anspach. East Lansing, MI: Michigan State University Press, 2013.

———. *Battling to the End: Conversations with Benoît Chantre.* Translated by Mary Baker. East Lansing, MI: Michigan State University Press, 2010.

———. *Deceit, Desire, and the Novel: Self and Other in Literary Structure.* Translated by Yvonne Freccero. Baltimore, MD: Johns Hopkins University Press, 1966.

———. *"To double business bound": Essays on Literature, Mimesis, and Anthropology.* Baltimore, MD: Johns Hopkins University Press, 1978.

———with Pierpaolo Antonello and João Cezar de Castro Rocha. *Evolution and Conversion: Dialogues on the Origins of Culture.* London: Continuum, 2008.

———. *I See Satan Fall Like Lightning.* Translated by James G. Williams. Maryknoll, NY: Orbis, 2001.

———. *Job: The Victim of His People.* Translated by Yvonne Freccero. Stanford, CA: Stanford University Press, 1987.

———. *Mimesis and Theory: Essays on Literature and Criticism, 1953–2005*. Edited by Robert Doran. Stanford, CA: Stanford University Press, 2008.

———. *Oedipus Unbound: Selected Writings on Rivalry and Desire*. Edited by Mark R. Anspach. Stanford, CA: Stanford University Press, 2004.

———. *The One by Whom Scandal Comes*. Translated by M.B. DeBevoise. East Lansing, MI: Michigan State University Press, 2014.

———. *Resurrection from the Underground: Feodor Dostoevsky*. Edited and translated by James G. Williams. East Lansing, MI: Michigan State University Press, 2012.

———. *Sacrifice*. Translated by Matthew Pattillo and David Dawson. East Lansing, MI: Michigan State University Press, 2011.

———. *The Scapegoat*. Translated by Yvonne Freccero. Baltimore, MD: Johns Hopkins University Press, 1986.

———. *A Theater of Envy: William Shakespeare*. New York: Oxford University Press, 1991.

———. *Things Hidden since the Foundation of the World*. Translated by Stephen Bann and Michael Metteer. Stanford, CA: Stanford University Press, 1987.

———. *Violence and the Sacred*. Translated by Patrick Gregory. Baltimore, MD: Johns Hopkins University Press, 1977.

———. *When These Things Begin: Conversations with Michel Treguer.* Translated by Trevor Cribben Merrill. East Lansing, MI: Michigan State University Press, 2014.

Index

Abel, 62–63
adulthood of humanity, 98–100
American Tobacco Company, 31–32
animals
  behavior of, 16, 39
  culture-making, 16, 26
  difference between humans and, 18, 62
  domestication of, 61
  sacrifice of, 62–63, 65, 90
apocalypse, 83, 98
Ascension, 107, 109–110
Augustine, 54, 110–111
autonomy, 9, 32–33, 41, 97n10, 99

Babylon 5, 97
Baptism, 22, 89, 112
Bernays, Eddie, 31–32
biblical religion, 11, 44, 53–54, 57, 101
Burgis, Luke, 31–32, 34–36, 102–103

Cain, 62–63, 117
cancel culture, 45, 85, 119

capitalism, 15, 87
catharsis, 48–49, 61n19, 79, 109
Celebristan, 34–38, 92, 110
charity, 90–91, 105, 110
cities, 14, 63, 117–118
colonization, 115–116
communion of saints, 105
contagion
  definition of, 43
  diffusion of, 102–103
  as Satan, 53–54
controlling violence, 63, 66, 75, 83–84, 87
conversion
  of Girard, 8–9
  and mimesis, 101–102, 114
Conversion of Saint Paul (Parmigianino), 114–115, 117–119
culture
  definition of, 14–16
  foundation of, 56–64
  transmission of, 26–27

Damascus, 117
Daswa, Benedict, 49–51
David, 68

INDEX

Dávila, Nicolás Gómez, 116
Day of Atonement, 44
"death of the gods," 109
demythologization, 11, 62,
    96–98, 101, 106–107
Derrida, Jacques, 10, 59n9
desire. *See* mimetic desire
differentiation, 111–113
distance
    from God, 107, 110–111
    and mediation, 34–37
double mediation, 30, 39–41
double transference/
    transformation, 59–60, 72,
    80, 106, 118

empathy, 102
end of history, 95
Enlightenment, 9n14, 15, 56,
    98–99
escalation to the extremes, 40
evil
    as nonbeing, 54–55
    problem of, 12, 15–16
evolution
    and culture, 16, 19
    and scapegoat mechanism, 52
existence
    and autonomy, 32–33
    human, 20–22
external mediation, 30, 34–37,
    66, 92, 110

forgiveness, 75, 98, 101
Francis (pope), 14, 88

freedom
    and mimesis, 101
    and will of God, 107–108
free speech, 45–46, 99
Freshmanistan, 34–38, 92
Fukuyama, Francis, 95
fulfillment stories, 103–104

Gaudium et Spes (Vatican II), 94
globalization, 85, 92–93, 115
gods, ancient, 53–55, 74, 80,
    106, 109
Gospel
    definition of, 80
    and history, 84–86, 96–100
    and scapegoat mechanism,
    72–76
guilt
    and forgiveness, 113
    of scapegoat, 43, 45, 49, 60,
    76

Habsburg dynasty, 115–118
Hegel, 58, 95–96
Hitchens, Christopher, 76
Hölderlin, Freidrich, 108–109
Holy Spirit, 2, 70, 73–74,
    78–82, 105, 113
hope, 94, 97–98, 100
human violence, 62, 108–109

identification, 111–113
imitatio Christi, 105–107
individualism, 9n14, 18, 31, 87
infancy, 99

INDEX

innocence
  of Jesus, 72–75, 79, 81, 111–113
  of the scapegoat, 72–73, 76, 80, 98
internal mediation, 30, 34–37, 92
intraspecies violence. *See* unbounded violence

Kant, Immanuel, 98–99
katéchon
  definition of, 65–66
  in history, 84–87, 96
Kennedy, Anthony, 32–33

language, 57–58
liberalism, 9n14, 45–46, 96

Marcion, 71
Marx, Karl, 15–16, 96
méconnaissance. See misapprehension
mediation
  double, 30, 39–41
  external vs. internal, 30, 34–37
mediator. *See* model
metaphysical poverty, 30, 32
mimetic contagion. *See* contagion
mimetic desire
  definition of, 8–9, 18–19
  and distance, 34–35
  of Israelites, 67
  and prohibitions, 61
  and rivalry, 39–40, 64, 92

thin vs. thick, 103
mimetic rivalry
  in Cain and Abel, 62–64
  as contagion, 43
  definition of, 39–41
  with God, 107–111, 113
  individual vs. societal, 64, 95
  Satan as, 55
mimetic violence, 55, 96, 101
misapprehension, 49, 58–61, 66, 79
model
  being/existence of, 30
  Christ as, 82, 105, 110
  in double mediation, 39–43
  in Freshmanistan and Celebristan, 34–38, 110
  vs. "other" and "mediator," 28–30
model-obstacle, 105
modernity, 9, 32, 36, 57, 85–89, 92, 99
murder
  in Cain and Abel, 62–64
  founding, 52–55, 58, 63
  and innocence, 72–78
  of Jesus, 72–78
  and myth, 58–61
myth
  founding of, 63
  and historical events, 58, 63
  and ideology, 96
  and power to conceal victims, 61, 65, 76
  of progress, 96
  See also misapprehension

mythology, 60–61, 108, 113
nature
   and culture, 16, 43, 84
   and essence, 19–21
natural catastrophe, 84
negative mimesis, 100–101, 105
New Commandment, 90, 106, 110
New Testament, 24, 54–55, 70–71

object of desire, 28–30, 92
Oedipus, 43, 48, 58–60
Old Testament, 12, 24, 65–71, 81, 90
other. *See* model

Pakaluk, Michael, 3
Paraclete, 2, 73, 79–82, 107, 116, 119
Parmigianino, 114, 117–119
Paschal Mystery, 2, 73, 84, 108, 112
Passion. *See* Paschal Mystery
Paul the Apostle. *See* Saul (New Testament)
peace
   absence of, 79, 85
   in the Holy Spirit, 70, 113
   maintaining, 49, 61, 66, 89, 111
   offered by Christ, 69, 74, 82, 98
   promoting, 15
   restoring, 60
Pentecost, 73, 80

persecution, 12, 60, 69–70, 74, 86n9, 96, 101
person. *See* subject
pharmakos, 10, 59, 61n19
plague, 43, 59–60, 93
Planned Parenthood v. Casey, 32
Plato, 10, 53, 59n9
polarization, 3
positive mimesis, 98, 100, 106, 110
prohibition, 1, 38, 55–56, 61–62, 66, 109, 111
prophets, 20, 63, 68–70, 81, 85

reciprocity, 40, 100–101, 110
reconciliation
   absence of, 79
   opportunity for, 99, 103, 111
   in scapegoat mechanism, 49, 56–59, 84–85
religion
   archaic, 57, 62, 65, 74, 86, 97, 101, 106
   biblical, 44, 53, 57, 101
   critique of, 76–77
   and culture, 15, 55, 62
   and politics, 14–17
   as result of scapegoat mechanism, 52–55
   See also sacred
revolution
   of Christ, 75, 78, 80
   French, 95
   variety of, 87, 88
righteousness, 49, 60, 80, 112–113

ritual
  repetition, 52, 56–58
  sacrifice, 56–58, 63
  of scapegoat, 44–47
Romantic lie, 9, 18, 31–33

sacred
  and Christ, 80–81, 83, 107–109
  corrupted, 102, 109
  creation of, 53–55
  exposure of, 70, 96–97
  as mother of all culture, 57
  and Saul's conversion, 117–118
  vs. secular, 62
  violent, 74, 77, 107, 110–111
sacrifice
  Christian, 77
  Eucharistic, 90
  human, 52, 64–65
  ritual, 56–58, 63
  spiritual, 65
Samaria, 68–69
Satan
  existence of, 53–55, 79
  as personification of scapegoat mechanism, 106, 117–118
  See also contagion
Saul (New Testament), 74, 98, 114, 117–119
Saul (Old Testament), 67–68
scandal, 39–41, 54, 64, 105, 118–119
scapegoating
  concealment of, 61
  as consequence of mimetic desire, 27
  crowd/community, 57, 59, 74
  definition of, 44–48
  dependence on, 89
  earliest form of, 52–55
  event of, 56, 58, 60, 70, 72, 111
  failure of, 48–49, 85
  ineffectiveness of, 84, 86, 96, 109
  and the *katéchon*, 64–66
  and misapprehension, 79, 81–82
  religion and, 76–77
  as response to violence, 64
  and Zeus, 108n14
scapegoat mechanism
  creative potential of, 65, 96
  definition of, 48–51
  and deified victim, 53
  and human evolution, 52
  positive effects of, 49
  and the Resurrection, 72–78
  revelation of, 51, 72, 96
  and the sacred, 53–55
  and Satan, 106, 117–118
  as solution to violence, 17, 39, 47
  See also biblical religion
Schwager, Raymund, 12, 77
Scripture, 21, 55, 71, 114
Second Coming, 84, 99
Second Vatican Council, 94
secularization, 57, 106

self-destruction, 2, 47, 84, 93, 96
September 11, 76
silence of God, 109
single victim mechanism. *See* scapegoat mechanism
snowballing, 64
social contagion. *See* contagion
Solomon, 29, 68
stoning, 52–53
subject, 28–30, 34, 39–40, 97n10
sympathy, 102, 116–117

taboo. *See* prohibition
Taylor, Charles, 105
Time Zone (artist), 94–95
totality, 58
transcendence
  of ancient myths, 106
  of bodily existence, 20–21
  of God, 107, 109, 111
triangular desire, 28–30
Trinity, 79
truth-telling, 75–76, 86, 118

unbounded violence, 17, 39, 52, 64

variability of the scapegoat, 48–49
vengeance, 62–63, 74, 86, 98, 113, 118
victim
  deified, 53
  expulsion of, 1, 58–59, 63, 111
  guilt of, 49, 57, 60, 73, 79, 86
  innocence of, 44, 72–78
  modern concern for, 2, 77, 88–92
  sacrificial, 57
victimization, 44, 46, 116
victimizers, 77–78, 85, 115
Vienna, 6n2, 115
violence
  controlling, 63, 66, 75, 83–84, 87
  and God, 70–71, 82, 98
  human, 62, 108–109
  and law, 97n9
  mimetic, 55, 96, 101
  as result of mimetic rivalry, 39–43, 111–112
  unbounded, 17, 39, 52, 64
  See also scapegoat mechanism
violent contagion, 79, 83, 97

withdrawal of God, 107–110
world destruction, 95
worship, 14–15, 54, 67–69

Yom Kippur, 44

Zeus, 108n14